914.11 Yomtov
Scotland

09/13/2014

Scotland

Scotland

BY NEL YOMTOV

Enchantment of the World™
Second Series

CHILDREN'S PRESS®

An Imprint of Scholastic Inc.

New York Toronto London Auckland Sydney
Mexico City New Delhi Hong Kong
Danbury, Connecticut

Frontispiece: **Isle of Hoy, Orkney Islands**

Consultant: Gary West, PhD, Senior Lecturer in Scottish Ethnology and Director of the
European Ethnological Research Center, University of Edinburgh, Scotland
Please note: All statistics are as up-to-date as possible at the time of publication.

Book production by The Design Lab

Library of Congress Cataloging-in-Publication Data
Yomtov, Nelson.
 Scotland / by Nel Yomtov.
   pages cm. — (Enchantment of the world)
 Includes bibliographical references and index.
 ISBN 978-0-531-20794-9 (library binding)
 1. Scotland—Juvenile literature. I. Title.
 DA762.Y66 2014
 941.1—dc23   2014001866

1 2 3 4 5 6 7 8 9 10 R 24 23 22 21 20 19 18 17 16 15

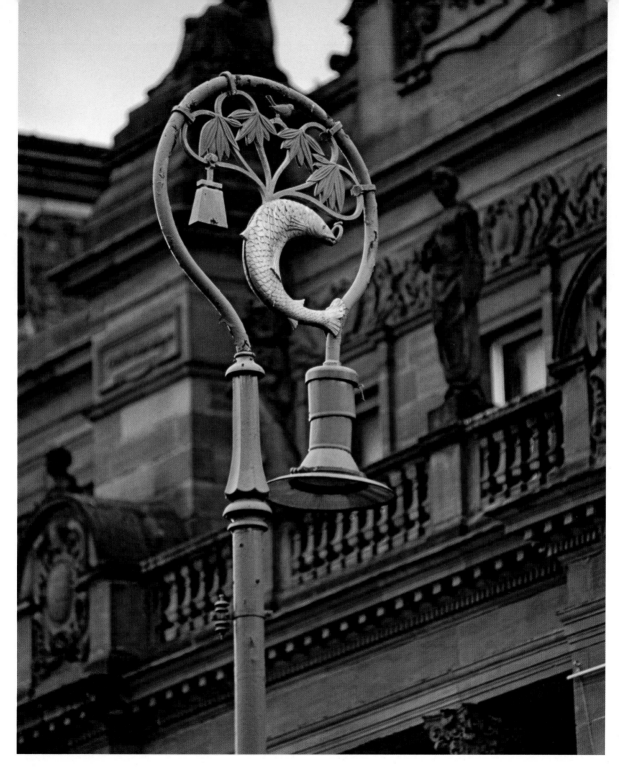

Lamppost, Glasgow

Contents

Left to right: **Fishing, bagpipes, Edinburgh, soccer fans, Eilean Donan Castle**

CHAPTER 1

A Land of Treasures

THE HAPPIEST LOT ON EARTH IS TO BE BORN A *Scotsman. You must pay for it in many ways, as for all other advantages on earth. But somehow life is warmer and closer; the hearth warms more redly; the lights of home shine softer on the rainy street; the very names, endeared in verse and music, cling nearer round our hearts.*

—Robert Louis Stevenson, 19th-century Scottish author of *Treasure Island* and *The Strange Case of Dr. Jekyll and Mr. Hyde*

Scotland is a land of treasures. It boasts rolling hills, rugged mountains, mysterious lakes, craggy coastlines, and remote islands. For thousands of years, Scotland's beauty and natural resources have lured adventurers to its shores. The first to arrive were hunter-gatherers and fishers from England and mainland Europe. These peoples were followed by Celtic tribes, Britons, Scots from Ireland, Romans, and Vikings from Denmark and Norway.

Opposite: **The dramatic, rocky Isle of Jura lies off the west coast of mainland Scotland.**

Scottish Lowland families fought English forces in the Battle of Otterburn in 1388.

For centuries, the country was not unified. Many different languages were spoken in the land. Mountains in the north sharply divided Scotland into two separate regions, the Highlands and the Lowlands. Rival groups from the two regions often fought each other. The Highlanders themselves split into warring families called clans. After years of political tension and bitter combat, Scotland joined with England to form the United Kingdom in 1707. Since that time, there has been peace in Scotland.

With peace came prosperity—and tourists from all parts of the world. About 15 million overnight trips are taken to Scotland each year. Visitors flock to attractions such as the Scottish National Portrait Gallery and Edinburgh Castle in Edinburgh, Scotland's capital. Glasgow, the country's largest city, offers tourists destinations such as the Kelvingrove Art Gallery and Museum and the Glasgow Cathedral. For lovers of the outdoors, walkers and hill climbers can travel to the Highlands to enjoy nature at its best. Loch Ness in the

A woman views displays at the Scottish National Portrait Gallery in Edinburgh.

Highlands is one of Scotland's deepest lakes—and is famed as the home of Nessie, the legendary Loch Ness Monster!

Scotland: a place of song, folklore, and fable; home to writers and poets, soldiers, and brilliant minds in science, invention, and philosophy. This land and its culture call to us in the patriotic song "Scotland the Brave":

High in the misty Highlands,
Out by the purple islands.
Brave are the hearts that beat beneath Scottish skies,
Wild are the winds to meet you.
Staunch are the friends that greet you,
Kind as the love that shines from fair maidens' eyes.

Purple heather and other shrubs bring splashes of color to the bleak landscape of the Highlands.

CHAPTER 2

A Charming Land

SCOTLAND IS LOCATED ON THE NORTHERN THIRD of the island of Great Britain. The island includes three of the four members of the United Kingdom—England, Wales, and Scotland. The fourth member, Northern Ireland, lies only 12 miles (19 kilometers) across the Irish Seas from Scotland.

Scotland is bordered on the south by England, with which it shares a 96-mile (155 km) border; on the east by the North Sea; and on the north and west by the Atlantic Ocean. The River Tweed marks the Scotland-England border in the southeast, and the Cheviot Hills set the border in the west and south.

In total area, Scotland covers 30,414 square miles (78,772 square kilometers), including nearly 800 surrounding islands, of which 130 are inhabited. The islands range in size from tiny parcels of rock to the Isle of Skye, which is about half the size of the U.S. state of Rhode Island.

Opposite: **Stone fences border many small farms on the Isle of Skye.**

A lighthouse warns ships away from the dangerous rocks of Cape Wrath. The light is visible 25 miles (40 km) out to sea.

From its northernmost tip at Cape Wrath to its border with England, Scotland's mainland is only 274 miles (441 km) long, and its greatest width is only 154 miles (248 km). Most places in Scotland are less than 45 miles (72 km) from the North Sea or the Atlantic Ocean.

The geography of Scotland can be neatly divided into three main land regions: the Highlands, the Central Lowlands, and the Southern Uplands.

The Highlands

The Highlands accounts for roughly two-thirds of Scotland. The region is dominated by two major mountain ranges, the Northwest Highlands and the Grampian Mountains. Glen More separates the two ranges. Both ranges extend northeast

Scotland's Geographic Features

Area: 30,414 square miles (78,772 sq km)

Highest Elevation: Ben Nevis, 4,409 feet (1,344 m)

Lowest Elevation: Sea level, along the coast

Longest River: River Tay, 117 miles (188 km)

Largest Lake: Loch Lomond, 27 square miles (70 sq km)

Average High Temperature: In Edinburgh, 45°F (7°C) in January, 66°F (19°C) in July

Average Low Temperature: In Edinburgh, 35°F (2°C) in January, 53°F (12°C) in July

Average Annual Precipitation: 28 inches (71 cm) in Edinburgh

Lowest Recorded Temperature: −17°F (−27°C), at Braemar, Grampian Mountains, February 11, 1895

Highest Recorded Temperature: 91°F (33°C), at Greycrook, Scottish Borders, August 9, 2003

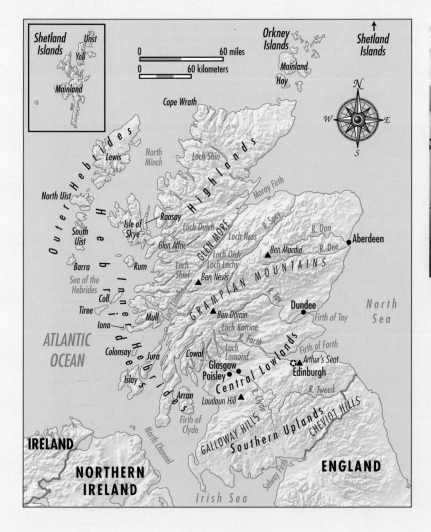

to southwest, with the largest mountains along the west coast. The Northwest Highlands offers spectacular scenery, but its steep hills and rocky soil make the region unfit for farming. Great Britain's two highest elevations—Ben Nevis at 4,409 feet (1,344 meters) and Ben Macdui, at 4,295 feet (1,309 m)—lie in the Grampians. Rich vegetation on the gentler slopes in the southern and eastern parts of the Grampians make the region home to extensive sheep and cattle raising. The region's glacier-carved mountains and plunging valleys create some of Scotland's most dramatic and imposing scenery. The Highlands is a favorite destination of hiking enthusiasts.

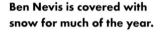

Ben Nevis is covered with snow for much of the year.

Scottish Geology Terms

Scots use their own terms for natural geologic formations. Here are just a few:

ben	mountain peak
brae	slope or hill
burn	stream
firth	an estuary, or narrow inlet, in the sea
glen	a narrow valley
loch	lake
moor	large tract of open, uncultivated land
strath	a broad, flat mountain valley

The Central Lowlands

The southern edge of the Grampians provides a natural boundary between the Highlands and the Central Lowlands. The Lowlands is a narrow band that stretches east to west just below the center of the country. It covers about one-tenth of the area of Scotland. The Lowlands is made up of low, rolling hills, rich farmland, and broad river valleys formed by ancient volcanic activity. Arthur's Seat, a peak rising to 822 feet (251 m), was formed by an extinct volcano system more than 350 million years ago. The area is home to large coalfields and iron deposits that were the hub of Scotland's early industrial growth in the 1800s. Many industrial villages still dot the region. About 75 percent of Scotland's population lives in the Central Lowlands. The country's two largest cities—Glasgow and Edinburgh, the capital—are located there.

The Southern Uplands

The Southern Uplands features several low ranges of hills, with elevations up to 2,750 feet (838 m). The uplands is a mainly rural and agricultural region with fertile plains and large areas of forest. Its natural beauty makes it a popular tourist and hill-walker destination. The area known as the Scottish Borders marks Scotland's boundary with England. The Southern Lowlands is the least populated of Scotland's three major geographic areas.

Lochs and Rivers

In Scotland, lakes are called *lochs* (pronounced "locks"). Most lochs are long and slender, tucked away in mountain valleys. The melting of glaciers about ten thousand years ago formed the lochs. Many of Scotland's lakes are hundreds of feet deep. The largest lake is Loch Lomond, which lies on the southern edge of the Highlands. With a surface area of 27 square miles (70 sq km), it is the largest freshwater lake in Great Britain. Loch Lomond is the subject of a well-known eighteenth-century song called "The Bonnie Banks o' Loch Lomond":

Munro's Namesakes

A Munro is any mountain in Scotland higher than 3,000 feet (914 m). The name comes from Sir Hugh Munro (1856–1919), a mountain climber who published a list of Scotland's 3,000-foot (914 m) mountains in 1891. His list, known as Munro's Tables, contained nearly three hundred peaks that topped this height. Until that time, mountaineers believed there were only about thirty. Today, many hikers try to climb all of Munro's mountains.

Oh! Ye'll take the high road,
And I'll take the low road,
And I'll be in Scotland afore ye.
But me and my true love will never meet again,
On the bonnie, bonnie banks of Loch Lomond.

The most famous of Scotland's lakes is Loch Ness, along Glen More. Loch Ness, Scotland's deepest lake at 745 feet (227 m), is sometimes said to be home to a mysterious animal—the Loch Ness Monster. Reports of a giant, dinosaur-like creature living in the lake date back to the 500s. Frequent scientific surveys of the lake, however, have failed to prove its existence. Yet tourists continue to flock to the site, hoping for a glimpse of the beast affectionately called Nessie.

Other lakes in Glen More include Loch Lochy, Scotland's third-deepest lake; Loch Linnhe on the west coast; and Loch Oich. Another major lake is Loch Katrine, which provides drinking water for Glasgow and its surrounding areas.

Scotland has twenty-six rivers that flow directly into the seas. Two major rivers, the Tay and the Forth, flow into the North Sea. The River Tay, at 117 miles (188 km) in length, is Scotland's largest river. It flows from the western Highlands, through the center of Scotland, and empties into a body of water called the Firth of Tay. To the south, the River Forth, which also originates in the Highlands, flows eastward into the Firth of Forth.

The River Clyde, Scotland's third-longest river, originates in the central Southern Uplands. It flows northwest past Glasgow and empties into the Atlantic Ocean. Historically, the Clyde has played a key role in Scotland's economic devel-

Dundee is the largest city on the River Tay.

opment. It is home to the nation's shipbuilding industry as well as the major waterway into Glasgow. Other significant rivers include Scotland's second-longest river, the River Spey, in the northeast; the River Dee in the southwest; and the River Tweed, which flows through the scenic Scottish Borders region in the south.

Stromness is the second-largest town in the Orkney Islands, with a population of about 2,190. The town dates back to the sixteenth century.

Islands

Most of Scotland's nearly eight hundred islands are found off the north and west coasts. The islands are generally divided into three groups: the Orkney Islands in the north, the Shetland Islands in the extreme north, and the Hebrides in the west.

The Orkney Islands lie roughly 7 miles (11 km) north of Caithness County. Of the roughly seventy Orkneys, about twenty are inhabited. The earliest known human settlement in the Orkneys dates back about nine thousand years. In the eighth and ninth centuries, Vikings from Denmark and

Norway used the islands as their base for invading mainland Scotland. Today, farming, tourism, and fishing are the main sources of income for the more than twenty-one thousand people who live in the Orkneys. Three-quarters of them reside on the largest of the Orkneys, called Mainland.

The Shetland Islands lie about 50 miles (80 km) northeast of the Orkneys. Of the one hundred islands, only sixteen are inhabited. The largest of the Shetlands is also called Mainland. Human activity on the Shetlands dates to about 4320 BCE. By the ninth century CE Vikings colonized the region. In the late twentieth century, the discovery of oil in the seas east and west of the Shetlands gave the islands a huge economic boost. Today, fishing, oil and natural gas, and tourism are the major industries there. About twenty-three thousand people live in the Shetlands.

Scotland's largest group of islands is the Hebrides. About five hundred islands make up the Hebrides, although many of them are only tiny rocky islands. The Hebrides is divided into two groups: the Inner Hebrides and the Outer Hebrides. The Inner Hebrides, which includes thirty-six inhabited islands, lies closer to mainland Scotland. The Isle of Skye is the largest and northernmost island of the Inner Hebrides. It is connected to the mainland by a bridge, built in 1995. Other islands of the Inner Hebrides include Jura, Iona, Mull, and Raasay. The Outer Hebrides includes fifteen inhabited islands. Lewis is the largest island of them, and home to roughly nineteen thousand people. In total, the Hebrides is home to nearly forty-seven thousand people.

Climate

Scotland has a temperate but varied climate. Much of Scotland, particularly the west coast, is warmed by the Gulf Stream, a current of warm air that flows from the Gulf of Mexico across the Atlantic Ocean to the British Isles. As a result, most of Scotland has fairly moderate temperatures, even in winter. In Glasgow and Edinburgh, for example, the average low temperature in January is around 35 degrees Fahrenheit (2 degrees Celsius). Moscow, Russia—which lies about as far north as these two cities but inland—has an average low in January of 16°F (–9°C)! In August, the average high temperature in Scotland is about 64°F (18°C).

A couple strolls along the beach in Morar, a village on the west coast of Scotland that is famous for its white sand beaches.

A thick blanket of snow covers the ground near Lochcarron, in the western Highlands.

In the higher reaches of the Highlands, snow patches on the ground may be present year-round. The Highlands also experiences powerful winds that move in from the Atlantic Ocean. Ben Nevis is exposed to such blasts for more than half the year. These winds are especially fierce in the Orkney and Shetland Islands during winter, blowing nearly nonstop and contributing to below-freezing temperatures.

Rainfall varies widely across Scotland. Precipitation is heavier and more frequent along the western Highlands, with annual rainfall up to 180 inches (460 centimeters). On the west coast, it is not unusual for rain to fall as many as 265 days a year. In comparison, the east coast receives less than 34 inches (86 cm) each year. Blizzards are rare in Scotland, with snow falling in the east about twenty days a year, compared to only ten days a year on the warmer west coast.

Looking at Scotland's Cities

The beginnings of Glasgow as a city date back to the sixth century, when Saint Mungo founded a religious community on the banks of the River Clyde. Today, with a population of 589,900, Glasgow is Scotland's largest city and the nation's commercial and industrial hub. Glasgow's vast George Square, built in 1781, is the center of the city. Other points of interest include the fifteenth-century Glasgow Cathedral (right) and Provand's Lordship, the city's oldest house; the Glasgow Gallery of Modern Art; and the People's Palace and Winter Gardens, a museum that tells the story of the city from the mid-eighteenth century to the present.

Edinburgh, the capital, is the nation's second-largest city with a population of 468,720. It is followed by Aberdeen (below), which has a population of 201,680. Hunter-gatherers first settled the Aberdeen area about eight thousand years ago. Its first church was built in the late sixteenth century, when Saint Machar began work to convert the local people to Christianity. Located between

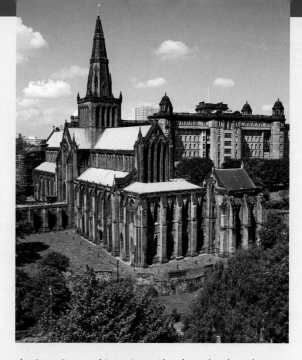

the River Dee and River Don, Aberdeen developed as an important fishing and trading settlement. Today, the oil industry is a major part of the local economy. Aberdeen is a beautiful city with fine sandy beaches, parks, gardens, and golf courses. On the cobbled streets of the city's oldest section, visitors can tour the ancient buildings of the University of Aberdeen, founded in 1495, as well as St. Machar's Cathedral.

The old seaport of Dundee, located in the eastern Central Lowlands on the Firth of Tay, is Scotland's fourth-largest city, with a population of 144,170. Dundee was long known for its textile industries and production of fruitcakes and jams. From the mid-nineteenth century to about 1920, the city was the homeport for steamships involved in the whaling industry. City landmarks include the City Churches and St. Mary's Tower, the oldest building in Dundee, built in the late fifteenth century. Several castles still remain, including Broughty Castle, which features displays on local history, arms and armor, and Dundee's past as a whaling port.

CHAPTER 3

Nature's Beauty

SCOTLAND'S PLANT AND ANIMAL LIFE VARY FROM region to region. Scotland has a diverse range of habitats, including seas, lowlands, mountains, rivers, lochs, and woodlands. Altogether, these various landscapes support roughly ninety thousand species of animals. About thirty of these species are endemic, meaning they are found nowhere else in the world.

Sea Life

Scotland's entire seacoast, including the islands and inlets, is roughly 10,250 miles (16,500 km) of waterfront. From open sea to inland freshwater lochs and rivers, Scotland's marine habitats teem with wildlife. More than forty thousand species of marine life make Scotland their home.

The seas surrounding Scotland are home to one-third of the world's whale and dolphin species. Orcas, also called killer whales, are among the fastest creatures in the sea—and among the most aggressive predators. Orcas are highly social animals. Several generations of orcas live together in groups called pods. Minke whales grow to an average of 24 feet (7 m) in length, with an average weight of about 5 tons (4.5 metric tons). They travel alone or in groups of two to four individuals. Bottlenose dolphins are found all around Scotland's coast. Moray Firth, in the North Sea, hosts a large colony of these mammals.

The harbor porpoise is found in shallow seas, particularly around the Hebrides and the northern islands. Common seals make their homes around shallow inland waters and estuar-

Harbor seals are highly social animals. They often relax on shore in small groups.

ies, and can often be found lying upon the rocky outcrops on the west coast. Scotland is home to about 90 percent of the United Kingdom's thirty-three thousand harbor seals. The gray seal also lives on Scotland's rockier west coast. About 120,000 gray seals inhabit the waters around Scotland.

Other forms of sea life found near Scotland include blue sharks, eels, sea bass, Atlantic halibut, rays, turtles, and dozens of varieties of shellfish and mollusks. The Darwin Mounds, off the northwest coast, are home to thriving colonies of colorful, often branching structures of deep-water coral. The coral provides a home to other marine life including, worms, sponges, starfish, and crabs.

About forty species of fish live in Scotland's freshwaters. They include shad, trout, eels, pike, perch, and minnow. Scottish rivers support one of Europe's largest populations of Atlantic salmon. At one time, Atlantic salmon was an important part of Scotland's fishing industry. Laws to protect against overfishing were enacted as early as 1318, and lawbreakers were severely punished.

A salmon leaps as it makes its way up the River Ettrick in the Scottish Borders region. Salmon are born in freshwater, spend their adult lives in the sea, and then return to the rivers where they were born to reproduce.

Red deer are among the largest deer species. Male red deer sometimes weigh more than 500 pounds (225 kg).

Mammals

About sixty species of mammal live wild in Scotland. Some of the species are in decline because of pollution, harmful agricultural practices, and overgrazing of pastureland.

The red deer is Scotland's most notable land animal, and the largest land animal in Great Britain. Thanks to government conservation efforts, the current population of red deer is roughly four hundred thousand, twice what it was in 1965. In spring, male red deer begin growing antlers, which can reach lengths of up to 45 inches (115 cm). Antlers can grow as fast as 1 inch (2.5 cm) per day! Most red deer live in the Highlands and northern islands, with large herds also found in the Galloway Hills in the Southern Uplands. At one time, reindeer roamed freely throughout Scotland, but they were hunted to near extinction. In recent years, small herds of reindeer have been reintroduced in the eastern Highlands.

About three-quarters of the United Kingdom's population of red squirrel are found in Scotland. With their tufted, furry ears and bushy tails, these small creatures are easy to spot. They are found in large numbers throughout the central Highlands and the forests of Dumfries and Galloway in the Southern Uplands. Scotland is also home to gray squirrels, pine martens, and harvest mice. The St. Kilda field mouse and the Orkney vole are found only in Scotland.

Other mammals found in Scotland include the European wildcat, wild goat, roe deer, mountain hare, European rabbit, and badger. About nine species of bat live in Scotland. The Daubenton's bat lives in woodland areas located near water. It swoops down close to the water and uses its large feet to grab prey from the surface.

Birds

About 250 species of bird are common in Scotland, including crows, woodpeckers, geese, grebes, and corncrakes. Birds of prey include the white-tailed sea eagle, the largest bird of prey in the United Kingdom. This majestic creature was

Scottish Wildlife Trust

The Scottish Wildlife Trust, Scotland's largest conservation group, manages 120 wildlife reserves. The organization works to preserve and restore natural wildlife habitats throughout the country. The trust has been instrumental in helping protect the red squirrel in Scotland.

hunted nearly to extinction in the nineteenth century. Since 1975, reintroduction programs have restored some of the population. White-tailed sea eagles now inhabit much of the Hebrides and mountain cliffs in the northwest parts of the Highlands. Other predator birds include ospreys, golden eagles, red kites, kestrels, owls, and peregrine falcons.

Scotland's waters are home to almost half of Europe's seabird population. In the summer, Arctic terns migrate from the frigid Antarctic to Scotland and other parts of the United Kingdom. The puffin is easily recognizable with its black head, large whitish cheeks, and brightly colored beak. In spring, puffins come ashore to breed in high sea cliffs and on coastal islands. They spend winters far out at sea. Measuring from 5 to 10 inches (13 to 25 cm), the storm petrel is the smallest of all seabirds. It usually nests in boulders and rocky outcroppings along the coast. Adventurous bird-watchers journey to the Shetland Islands where thousands of storm petrels breed each year. Some of the birds make their nests in an ancient, round stone tower called the Broch of Mousa.

National Tree: Scots Pine

The Scots pine is the national tree of Scotland. It is an evergreen, meaning it keeps its leaves in all four seasons. The Scots pine is easily recognized by its combination of short blue-green leaves and orange-red bark. At one time, the Scots pine formed most of the forestland in the Scottish Highlands. However, cutting down vast tracts of forest for timber and overgrazing by deer and sheep have greatly reduced the numbers of Scots pine in the region.

Plant Life

Human activity has stripped Scotland of much of its woodlands. In ancient times, the region was covered in thick forests. Over time, they were cut down to clear land for farming and grazing. Today, about 17 percent of Scotland is forested. Much of Scotland's woodlands are found in the Southern Uplands and in the Highlands. Typical trees include Scots pine, common juniper, Douglas fir, Norwegian spruce, and yew.

Peat bogs cover much of the Scottish landscape, particularly in the northern Highlands, western and northern islands, and low-lying wetlands. In these areas, rainfall and melting snow accumulate rather than run off. Peat moss thrives under these growing conditions, with new, live plants growing on top of beds of dead plants. Villagers cut the moss, allow it to dry, and then burn it as a fuel for heating and cooking. Peat bogs also serve as an important source of drinking water and as pastureland for grazing sheep.

Mountainsides support a large variety of plants and shrubs. Purple heather is a favorite among Scots and is widely grown in

Thick moss covers the ground in peat bogs. It can absorb large amounts of water, making the ground spongy.

A cow grazes in the heather of the Scottish Highlands.

home gardens. Sheep and deer graze on the tips of the plants. Bell heather, a low-growing shrub, produces flowers that are bell-shaped. Azaleas, pearlwort, mountain avens, club moss, and dwarf willow also grow high on mountains and cliffs.

Symbol of a Nation

It may only be a lowly prickly leaved weed, but the thistle has been the national emblem of Scotland since the thirteenth century. The thistle symbolizes courage and noble character. Images of thistles have long appeared on Scottish coins and heraldic badges. According to legend, a Norse soldier stepped on a thistle during a raid on a Scottish army's camp. The soldier cried out in pain, alerting the Scots to the presence of their enemy. The Scots defeated the Norse invaders, and the thistle was adopted as the symbol of Scotland.

The peat bogs of the Hebrides feature large pastures of plantago, a small, weed-like plant that includes the brightly colored sea thrift and the red fescue. The low-lying grassy plains on the Outer Hebrides include rare plant species such as yellow rattle and lady's tresses.

Homegrown Animals

Centuries ago, Scottish farmers and ranchers developed many breeds of animals. Most of the sheep in Scotland are called blackface sheep, or Scottish blackface. This type of sheep was

Blackface sheep are tough and hardy, able to survive the harsh weather in the Highlands.

likely first bred in the Southern Uplands. Its long, thick coats protect it against biting winds and cold temperatures. Blackface are raised mainly for their meat, and their wool is prized as mattress filling and fibers for clothing, carpets, and textiles.

The Shetland pony originated in the Shetland Islands. Growing only 28 to 42 inches (71 to 107 cm) tall, these small but hardy animals were once used to pull carts and plow farmland. They were also used to haul coal in underground coal mines in Great Britain and the United States. Today, Shetlands are used mainly for entertainment, serving

Shetland ponies tend to be gentle and good natured, making them popular for children.

Dogs of Scotland

Scotland has produced some of the world's most popular breeds of dog. The country's best-known breed is the Scottish terrier, or Scottie (left). This small dog originated in the Highlands. It was raised to herd sheep and hunt animals that destroyed crops, such as foxes and badgers. Scotties are one of five breeds of terrier from Scotland. The others are the Skye, cairn, Dandie Dinmont, and West Highland white terrier. Several breeds of collie hail from Scotland, including the Border collie from the Scottish Borders region and the Shetland sheepdog from the Shetland Islands. The golden retriever originated in the eighteenth century in Glen Affric, a village in the Highlands. Originally raised to assist bird hunters, these friendly, gentle dogs are now also used as guide dogs for the blind and for finding humans in search-and-rescue operations.

as mounts for small children at horse shows, riding schools, and local fairs. An organization in England, however, trains Shetlands to be guide animals for people who are blind or partly sighted. The Scots also developed the Clydesdale, one of the largest breeds of horse. Standing up to 6 feet (1.8 m) tall and weighing nearly 2,000 pounds (900 kilograms), this powerful workhorse is still used as it was centuries ago, pulling plows and hauling heavy items.

Among the breeds of beef cattle developed by the Scots are the Highland, the Aberdeen Angus, and the Ayrshire. The Galloway was developed in the Southern Uplands, and is now found in many parts of the world. The Galloway's thick, woolly coat makes it ideally suited to harsher, colder climates.

CHAPTER 4

Scotland the Brave

HUMANS HAVE INHABITED SCOTLAND FOR ABOUT ten thousand years. The first people to arrive in the region came from southern England or the European mainland. These early people were hunter-gatherers and fishers. They made tools of flint and built circular houses with stones. By roughly 4500 BCE, the area's inhabitants started to farm and raise cattle and sheep. These people built more permanent stone dwellings, many dome-shaped. They also used standing stones as monuments or sites of religious worship.

By about 1800 BCE, bronze was introduced to Scotland. People began crafting farm tools, weapons, and decorative statues with the metal. Evidence of these bronze workers can be found on the isles of Lewis and Brodgar in the Orkney Islands.

Celts Arrive

People called Celts moved into what is now Scotland from central Europe by about 500 BCE, bringing with them tools made of

Opposite: **Ancient people erected the Callanish Stones on the island of Lewis and Harris in the Outer Hebrides more than 4,500 years ago.**

a new and stronger metal, iron. The Celts also brought horses, plows, war chariots, new crops, and a highly developed religion based on many gods. Celtic tribes built huge forts on hilltops, as well as extraordinary stone towers called brochs, whose true purpose is still not known for certain to this day. For centuries, Celtic tribes battled one another until a common enemy, the Romans, invaded the British Isles in 43 CE. By this time, the Romans, based in Italy, controlled a vast empire that stretched across Europe, North Africa, and western Asia.

The Romans invaded Great Britain in 43 CE. They would rule parts of the island for more than 350 years.

Ancient Monuments

Near the small village of Stromness, on Mainland, the largest of the Orkney Islands, are the ruins of a nearly perfectly preserved prehistoric village. Known as Skara Brae (left), the village was inhabited around 3100 BCE, more than five thousand years ago. The site is made up of eight houses, including a large workshop where tools were made. Archaeologists have discovered furniture built with stone, including dressers, seats, shelves, and storage boxes. There is a primitive type of toilet in each house, as well as a system of drains under the floors for indoor sanitation. The village was abandoned around 2500 BCE—although no one knows why.

Another ancient monument in Scotland is the Callanish Stones. Located on the Isle of Lewis in the Outer Hebrides, this circle of thirteen stones is similar to another famous structure, Stonehenge, in England. The stones vary in size from about 3 to 15 feet (1 to 5 m) tall, forming a circle about 65 feet (20 m) in diameter. Archaeologists believe the stone circle was built between 2900 and 2600 BCE. The site was likely used for religious rituals or to calculate movements of the sun. One local tradition claims the stones are giants who once inhabited the island. When the giants refused to be converted to Christianity, they were turned to stone as punishment.

By 81 CE, the Romans had conquered the people of what is now England and had marched north into Scotland. The Romans and the northern Celts fought many bloody battles. The northerners painted their faces with fearsome designs to terrify opponents in war. The Romans named some of these tribes Picts, from the Latin word *picti*, meaning "painted."

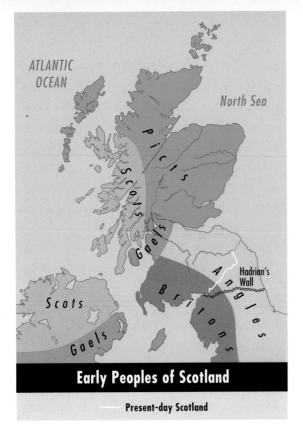

ATLANTIC OCEAN

North Sea

Picts

Scots

Gaels

Hadrian's Wall

Angles

Britons

Scots

Gaels

Early Peoples of Scotland

— Present-day Scotland

After driving the Picts into the Highlands, the Romans built a series of forts across the narrowest part of Scotland as protection. In the 120s, the Romans built a more permanent defensive structure farther south, in northern England. It was named Hadrian's Wall, after the Roman emperor Hadrian who ordered its construction. In the 400s, as Rome itself was facing foreign invasions, Roman troops withdrew from Britain and returned home.

Unifying a Kingdom

In the 400s, a Celtic tribe arrived from northern Ireland and established a stronghold on Scotland's west coast. The Romans called these people the Scotti, or Scots. These newcomers spoke an early form of modern Gaelic. In the following decades, missionaries from Ireland gradually spread Christianity to the Picts and Scots, who worshipped many gods. The most influential Christian monk was Saint Columba, who established a church on the island of Iona in the Inner Hebrides in 563. The Scots grew in number and power, and in 843, Kenneth MacAlpin, king of the Scots, also became king of the Picts, uniting the two kingdoms.

By this time, four major ethnic groups inhabited Scotland. The Picts occupied the northern islands and the north and east of the mainland. The Scots inhabited the western region. The last remaining Romanized British, called the Britons,

occupied the southwest, and the Angles, invaders from Germany, inhabited the southeast. A fifth group was about to emerge and help further shape the destiny of the kingdom.

In the eighth and ninth centuries, Viking invaders established settlements in the Shetland and Orkney Islands. Other bands arrived from areas the Vikings had conquered in Britain and Ireland. These groups settled in the Central Lowlands.

Different languages were spoken throughout Scotland. In the northern islands, the languages of Denmark and Norway were spoken. The wealthy spoke Scottish Gaelic, imported from Ireland. In the south, the Angles spoke Anglo-Saxon, the root of modern English.

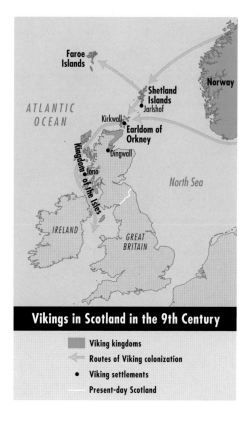

Vikings in Scotland in the 9th Century

- Viking kingdoms
- Routes of Viking colonization
- Viking settlements
- Present-day Scotland

For countless decades, Scots, together with their Pict allies, jostled Britons and Angles for dominance in Scotland. In 1005, Scots king Malcolm II came to power after defeating his cousin Kenneth III. In 1018, Malcolm defeated the Angles and seized their territories. Then he installed his grandson, Duncan, as king of the Britons. By 1034, the four groups—all Gaelic-speaking and Christian—were united. Duncan was king of all of Scotland, except for the Vikings' territories. In 1266, Norway would sell the Hebrides to Scotland, and in 1472 the Orkneys and Shetlands would become Scottish.

Malcolm II was the first Scottish king to rule over an area roughly similar in size to today's Scotland.

The English Invasion

In 1057, Malcolm III, known as "Big Head," became king of Scotland. Malcolm had grown up in England during the reign of a general-king named Macbeth, who had killed Malcolm's father, Duncan. Wishing to expand his kingdom into northern England, Malcolm's troops conducted raids across the border. In 1071, England's ruler, William the Conqueror, invaded Scotland and forced Malcolm to swear

his allegiance to him. After Malcolm's death in 1093, three of his sons ruled in succession. Within eighty years, Lowland Scotland became heavily influenced by England. The Celtic way of life was disappearing.

In 1165, William I, known as William the Lion because of his bravery and the design of his emblem—a red lion on a yellow background—became king of Scotland. At the time, England's Henry II ruled over Northumbria, the ancient homeland of the Angles. William wanted it back, and in 1174, he invaded England. William's forces were defeated and he was taken prisoner. He was forced to sign a treaty with Henry II that made Scotland a territory of England.

William the Lion (on fallen horse) was captured by English forces at the Battle of Alnwick in 1174.

Scottish forces battled English troops (on horseback) during the reign of King Edward I. Edward's attempt to subdue Scotland led to years of warfare.

Scotland and England were mostly at peace for the next century. But in 1295, English king Edward I—called the Hammer of the Scots—demanded money from the Scots to pay for England's wars with France. The Scots refused and instead made an alliance with the French. Edward was furious. The next year, English armies invaded Scotland, taking control of castles and towns in the south. Edward further humiliated the defeated Scots by taking the Stone of Destiny—the ancient stone slab on which Scottish kings where crowned—back to England.

Scotland was a defeated nation: Foreign troops occupied the south, and it appeared the country was on the verge of total domination by their English foes. But the Scots still had some fight left in them—and rebellion was soon to come.

The Wars of Independence

In 1297, William Wallace, the son of a minor Scottish nobleman, took command of a group of rebel Scots that were fighting English armies. At the town of Stirling on the River Forth, Wallace's forces soundly crushed an army of English

The Stone of Destiny

It looks simple enough: a rectangular block of sandstone that measures 26 inches (66 cm) long by 16 inches (41 cm) wide by 11 inches high (28 cm), and weighs about 336 pounds (152 kg). Carved on its top surface is a Latin cross. For centuries, this unusual stone sat in an abbey in the town of Scone, near Perth. A medieval legend said the prophet Jacob rested his head on the stone when he dreamed of angels ascending to heaven. Every Scot who was about to become king went to Scone to sit on the rock for the coronation ceremony that officially made him ruler of the land. The rock was called the Stone of Destiny, also known as the Stone of Scone. In 1296, King Edward I of England, the Hammer of the Scots, raided the abbey and took the sacred rock. He moved it to Westminster Abbey in London, where it remained for seven hundred years. In 1996, the stone was returned to Scotland by the British government (left). It now rests in an honored spot in Edinburgh Castle.

A massive statue of Robert the Bruce looms near the site of the Battle of Bannockburn.

knights. Soon Wallace and his band of warriors launched furious raids into the north of England, destroying and plundering as they went along. The next year, Wallace was defeated by King Edward's troops at Falkirk. Wallace escaped, but he was captured in 1305 and hanged.

The English, however, could not break the Scots' resistance. In 1306, Robert the Bruce was crowned king of Scotland. After the English destroyed his army near the city of Perth, Bruce went into hiding, planning his revenge. He assembled another army and crushed the English at Loudoun Hill in 1307. For the next several years, Bruce's growing army captured one English stronghold after another. In 1314, Bruce's forces destroyed the English army—led by King Edward II, son of the Hammer of the Scots—at the Battle of Bannockburn. Scotland had won its independence.

The Reformation in Scotland

Peace in the Scottish kingdom was short-lived. After Bruce's death in 1329, the English once again overran Scotland and were expelled only after years of bloody fighting. Whatever national unity had been achieved crumbled. Highland groups would sometimes attack villages in the Lowlands. Scotland was poor, and a series of weak kings threatened its stability.

In the late fifteenth century, however, things began to improve. James IV came to the Scottish throne in 1488 and began a series of reforms that reshaped the nation. He built universities and improved the legal system. Under his guidance, Scotland became more prosperous and capably governed. In 1503, James married Margaret Tudor, an English princess. It was hoped the marriage would bring a lasting peace between Scotland and England. But when England invaded France, James attacked England in recognition of Scotland's old alliance with the French. The English routed the Scots at Flodden Field, killing more than ten thousand Scots, including James IV.

In the sixteenth century, religious differences added to Scotland's woes. In Scotland, as throughout all of Europe, Roman Catholicism was the dominant religion and most influential cultural and social force in society. The Church owned huge amounts of land and grand cathedrals and abbeys. Only the Church had large numbers of people who could read and write. In 1517, a German monk named Martin Luther demanded that the Catholic Church reform, or change, its old ways. Luther's actions launched a movement called the Reformation, which introduced a new sect of Christianity called Protestantism. By the end of the century, half the people of Europe had adopted various Protestant faiths.

In Scotland, a one-time Catholic priest named John Knox led the Reformation. Influenced by Knox's fiery anti-Catholic speeches, mobs burned churches and destroyed abbeys. By 1560, the Scottish Parliament, led by Knox, outlawed the Catholic Church and established the Church of Scotland, a Presbyterian denomination. England also converted to Protestantism, while France remained Catholic.

During these years of chaos and turmoil, Mary, Queen of Scots rose to prominence. Mary became queen of Scotland when her father, James V, died. She was only six days old. As a young girl, Mary, a Catholic, was sent to France for safety. There she married, and after her husband died, she returned to Scotland in 1561 to rule the then Protestant nation. She remarried, but pressure from Protestant nobles forced Mary to give up the throne. She was imprisoned, but escaped and fled to London to seek the aid of her cousin, Queen Elizabeth I.

Elizabeth, fearing Mary would take the throne in England, had her cousin executed in 1587.

Union at Last

Before her death in 1603, Queen Elizabeth I named King James VI of Scotland—the son of Mary, Queen of Scots—as her successor. When Elizabeth died, James VI of Scotland also became King James I of England. James ruled England and Scotland from London, but the two countries remained separate.

Scots were divided on the idea of political unity with England. Some believed a single, unified Parliament would give the Scots a stronger voice in their own affairs. Others still felt anger toward England for the years of cruelty and warfare it had inflicted on Scotland. In 1707, however, the Scottish and English Parliaments agreed to the Treaty of Union, which brought England and Scotland together under one government. Scotland was no longer an independent nation.

King James I ruled over both England and Scotland for twenty-two years.

The English and Scottish Parliaments agreed to the Treaty of Union during the reign of Queen Anne. The Scottish Duke of Queensberry (kneeling) had been largely responsible for its acceptance in Scotland.

Opposition to Unity

Some Scots were outraged by the Treaty of Union. In 1714, Highland clans proclaimed James Edward Stuart to be king, rather than accepting George I, who was about to assume the throne. The next year, Highland rebels called Jacobites, meaning "followers of James," took up arms and launched a rebellion against the British. The British government crushed the Jacobite uprising at the Battle of Sheriffmuir, and James Edward Stuart fled to France.

To discourage further Jacobite rebellions, the government built forts and stationed troops in the Highlands. Undaunted, the Jacobites rose up once again in 1745. This time they were led by James's son Charles Edward Stuart, known as Bonnie

Prince Charlie. Charles led the Jacobites to several early victories against the government forces, and in seizing control of Edinburgh, Scotland's capital. He also invaded England itself. When French forces failed to join the Jacobites as Charles had hoped, the rebels returned home to Scotland. The final showdown between the Jacobites and the British government came in April 1746, at Culloden near Inverness, when the well-trained government force crushed the Jacobite army.

As punishment, the British government set out to finally destroy the rebel Highlanders' way of life. Government forces burned Highland villages, destroyed farmland, and slaughtered clan chiefs. Traditional Highland costumes were banned, and Highlanders were no longer allowed to carry weapons. Many clansmen warriors were made to serve in the British army.

Glenfinnan Monument

Located at Loch Shiel in the Scottish Highlands is a stone tower called the Glenfinnan Monument. The monument marks the spot where Charles Edward Stuart raised his flag on August 19, 1745, to announce the beginning of the second Jacobite rebellion. Alexander MacDonald, a local landowner, built the tower in 1815. In 1830, a huge statue of a man dressed in Highland clothing—perhaps Charles himself—was added atop the monument. The base of the statue features a plaque in three languages—Gaelic, Latin, and English—that explains the monument. Visitors are invited to climb to the top of Glenfinnan Monument for a breathtaking view of Loch Shiel and the surrounding glen.

R. B. Cunninghame Graham, a politician, writer, and journalist, was elected the first president of the Scottish National Party in 1934.

Aberdeen and Inverness prospered. In the years since, many of the old industries have continued to decline as high-tech industries and service industries such as tourism have grown.

Toward Greater Independence

In the twentieth century, some Scots began arguing that Scotland should become independent from the United Kingdom. The Scots believed that independence would bring about greater economic prosperity and political freedoms. The Scottish National Party (SNP) was formed in 1934 and grew in numbers and strength over time. In 1974, the SNP had eleven elected Members of Parliament.

By the late twentieth century, many Scots supported the idea called devolution. This would mean some self-rule for Scotland through a peaceful transfer of power from the British Parliament to the nation. Most Scottish supporters of devolution did not want a complete break from the United Kingdom. They favored a limited form of self-government for Scotland. In a 1979 referendum, only 33 percent of the Scots who voted favored devolution.

Scots voted on the issue again in 1997, and this time, they voted overwhelmingly for devolution. The Scotland Act 1998 established the new Scottish Parliament and outlined its powers and responsibilities. The Scottish Parliament began meeting the following year.

Some Scots continue to push for complete independence from the United Kingdom. Although polls in 2013 indicated that most Scots oppose independence, it is a question that people throughout Scotland ponder seriously.

Queen Elizabeth II (in purple jacket) enters the Scottish Parliament chamber on July 1, 1999, the first day the Scottish Parliament was in session in nearly three hundred years.

CHAPTER 5

A Young Government

I N 1998, THE PARLIAMENT OF THE UNITED KINGDOM, based in London, England, approved the establishment of the Scottish Parliament. The Scotland Act 1998 gave Scots a limited form of self-government.

Like the United Kingdom as a whole, the Scottish government is divided into three branches: executive, legislative, and judicial.

Executive Branch

The executive branch of the Scottish government, the branch responsible for running the government, is formally called the Scottish Government. The head of the Scottish Government is the first minister. He or she is nominated by the Scottish Parliament and appointed by the monarch of the United Kingdom, currently Queen Elizabeth II. The first minister appoints the members of his or her cabinet, but the selections must be approved by the Parliament. Each cabinet minister is in charge of a different department, such as health and well-being, education and lifelong learning, justice, cultural and external affairs, games and sport, and public health.

The monarch of the United Kingdom is the head of state and commander in chief of the armed forces. All acts of Parliament require her approval.

National Government of Scotland

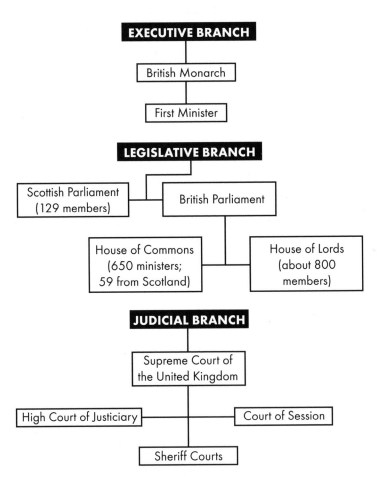

EXECUTIVE BRANCH

British Monarch

First Minister

LEGISLATIVE BRANCH

Scottish Parliament (129 members)

British Parliament

House of Commons (650 ministers; 59 from Scotland)

House of Lords (about 800 members)

JUDICIAL BRANCH

Supreme Court of the United Kingdom

High Court of Justiciary

Court of Session

Sheriff Courts

Legislative Branch

The Scotland Act 1998 spells out what the new Scottish Parliament—the nation's legislative branch—can and cannot do. The new Parliament can make laws in such areas as education, health, housing, farming, local government and courts, and taxes. It cannot negotiate treaties with other nations. Nor can it establish policies that relate to energy, national security, employment, social security, and a number of other areas.

The British Parliament in London continues to oversee and pass laws regarding these matters. The British Parliament is divided into two parts: the House of Commons and the House of Lords. The Commons is the main governing body in the United Kingdom. It has 650 members, 59 of whom are from Scotland.

First Minister Alex Salmond (standing) discusses issues with members of the Scottish Parliament in 2014.

Tony Blair, Son of Scotland

Born in Edinburgh in 1953, Tony Blair served as the prime minister of the United Kingdom from 1997 to 2007. Blair spent much of his childhood in Australia and Durham, England. He graduated from Oxford University with a degree in law in 1975 and joined the Labor Party, winning a seat in the British Parliament in 1983. Rising quickly through the party's ranks, Blair was elected leader of the Labor Party in 1994. Three years later, he was elected prime minister of the United Kingdom.

During his time in office, Blair introduced important reforms in education, health care, transportation, and workers' rights. Under his watch, public spending on social services increased, which helped to reduce poverty and homelessness in the United Kingdom.

Blair also strongly supported the U.S.-led wars that followed the terrorist attacks of September 11, 2001. Despite widespread opposition from the British public and members of Parliament, Blair supported the actions of U.S. president George W. Bush (above, right) and sent British troops to fight in both Afghanistan and Iraq. As British casualties mounted in the Iraq War, Blair's popularity dropped. As a result, in the 2005 elections, the Labor Party lost many seats in Parliament. Pressure from within the Labor Party eventually forced Blair to resign as head of the party and as prime minister in 2007.

The Scottish Parliament has 129 members who are elected to four-year terms. Each member represents a different district in the country. They are known as Members of the Scottish Parliament, or MSPs.

The most popular political party in recent years has been the Scottish National Party (SNP). The SNP, formed in 1934, is committed to Scottish independence. In 2014, it held 65 of the 129 seats in the Scottish Parliament. The Labor Party, once the most powerful party in modern Scottish politics, held 37 seats. The Conservative Party, the Liberal Democrats, and the Green Party are also active in Scotland.

Members of the Scottish National Party (SNP) pose in 2011 after winning a landslide victory in parliamentary elections. For the first time, the SNP held a majority of seats in the Scottish Parliament.

Scotland's Flag

Scotland's flag is based on the cross of Saint Andrew, also known as the Saltire. The flag consists of a white X-shaped cross on a blue background. According to legend, in about the year 750, a Pictish warrior-king named Unust (also known as Angus) was losing in battle to an Angles army. Suddenly, Saint Andrew appeared to Unust in a dream, promising the Picts victory. The Pict warriors later saw a cross-shaped formation of clouds in the sky. The cross shape was similar to the diagonal cross on which Saint Andrew is said to have been crucified. Inspired by these images, the Picts defeated the Angles in the important battle. Saint

Andrew was adopted as Scotland's patron saint, and the Saltire was adopted as the symbol of the Scottish nation.

Judicial Branch

Because the United Kingdom does not have a single, unified judicial system, Scottish law remained independent after the union of Scotland and England in 1707. Therefore, Scotland's legal system has its own set of laws, procedures, and policies.

The Supreme Court of the United Kingdom is the highest civil court of appeal in Scotland. Established in 2009, the Supreme Court is empowered to hear cases that involve the Scotland Act 1998. Occasionally, disputes arise regarding the legality of laws passed by the Scottish Parliament or the powers of the executive branch. The Supreme Court helps resolve these questions. The Court of Session is the highest civil court in Scotland. It deals with cases that involve challenging government decisions.

The High Court of Justiciary is Scotland's highest criminal court. It handles serious cases of crime involving murder and major drug offenses. It also hears appeals of criminal cases

National Anthem

"God Save the Queen" is the national anthem for the entire United Kingdom. Scotland itself does not have an official national anthem. Instead, several songs are used as unofficial anthems, including "Flower of Scotland." The song is often sung at rugby and soccer games. Roy Williamson, a member of the folk group the Corries, wrote the song in 1965.

Gaelic lyrics

O Fhlùir na h-Alba, cuin a chì sinn an seòrsa laoich?
A sheas gu bàs 'son am bileag feòir is fraoich.
A sheas an aghaidh feachd uailleil Iomhair.
'S a ruaig e dhachaidh air chaochladh smaoin.

English lyrics

O Flower of Scotland, when will we see your like again?
That fought and died for your wee bit hill and glen.
And stood against him, Proud Edward's army.
And sent him homeward to think again.

A man leaves a sheriff's court in Oban. Sheriff courts deal with both civil and criminal matters.

from lower courts. The judges who make up the High Court of Justiciary are the same ones who sit in the Court of Session.

Scotland is divided into six regional judicial districts called sheriffdoms. There are forty-nine sheriff courts spread throughout the sheriffdoms. A judge, called a sheriff, hears cases that deal with less serious offenses.

Local Government

Scotland is divided into thirty-two councils, which are responsible for services such as sanitation, running elections, and other community matters. The councils vary in population, from Glasgow City with about six hundred thousand residents, to Orkney, which has only about twenty-one thousand inhabitants. Council members are elected to four-year terms.

A Look at the Capital

Edinburgh, Scotland's capital and second-largest city, lies on the southern shore of the Firth of Forth. It is home to roughly 470,000 people. The city is divided into several districts. Among them, Old Town, on the south side, is the ancient heart of Edinburgh, with its dark, cobbled medieval streets. New Town, lying to the north, features wide streets planned around a network of lush parks, gardens, and public squares. Edinburgh Castle lies on the Royal Mile in Old Town. Human settlement at the site dates back at least three thousand years, with the first fort built on the site around 600 CE. The castle houses the National War Museum of Scotland and the Stone of Destiny. Other sites in Old Town include the Scottish Parliament, the National Museum of Scotland, and the Palace of Holyroodhouse, the queen's official residence in Scotland.

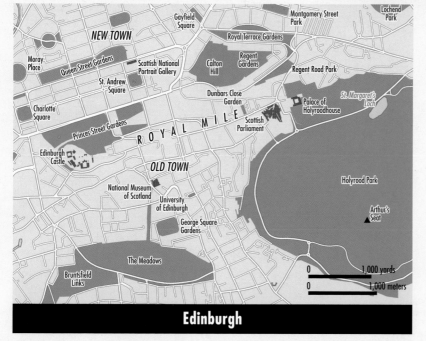

Edinburgh boasts the second-strongest economy of any city in the United Kingdom, behind London. Its main industries are banking and other financial services, scientific research, education, and tourism. The city is also the center of Scotland's government and legal system.

Since 2001, the proportion of people living in Edinburgh who were born outside the United Kingdom has almost doubled. The largest numbers of newcomers hail from Poland, China, India, and Pakistan.

CHAPTER 6

A Diverse Economy

From the Industrial Revolution until the mid-twentieth century, Scotland's economy was dominated by heavy industry, such as shipbuilding, iron and steel production, and coal mining. These industries declined in the 1970s and 1980s, leading to a shift in the economy toward technology and services, including finance and tourism. Scotland's economy received a big boost from the discovery of huge reserves of oil and natural gas in the North Sea. Today, Scotland's economy continues to grow, and its unemployment rate is the lowest in the United Kingdom.

Opposite: **Scotland has been producing fine textiles for centuries.**

Manufacturing

Manufacturing accounts for about 25 percent of Scotland's gross domestic product (GDP), the total value of the goods and services produced in the country. The country's long history of textile manufacturing continues today in modern factories, where clothing, hats, gloves, and other accessories are produced.

Workers unload windows that will be installed in a new hotel in Edinburgh.

The Scottish Borders council area in southeastern Scotland is home to many companies that produce high-quality knitted goods, particularly in towns like Galashiels, Hawick, and Innerleithen. Weavers in the Outer Hebrides produce Harris tweed, from wool that is dyed and spun locally. Many weavers work from home. The tweed is exported to international markets where it is sewn into high-quality jackets.

Scotland's construction industry provides about 170,000 jobs, or about 10 percent of all Scottish jobs. The worldwide economic crisis of 2007–2008 significantly hurt Scotland's construction industry. By 2011, however, construction showed signs of a strong rebound to precrisis numbers.

Scotland's Silicon Glen in the Central Belt between Glasgow and Edinburgh is home to a small but growing electronics industry. In the 1980s and 1990s, Silicon Glen was home to companies such as Texas Instruments, Motorola, Sun Microsystems, and NCR, which manufactured personal computers, computer parts, computer notebooks, and automated teller machines (ATMs). Today, electronics design and development companies include IBM, National Semiconductor, and Freescale Semiconductor. Software development is becoming increasingly more important in Silicon Glen. Among the industry leaders based there are Amazon.com and Rockstar North, the developer of the computer game *Grand Theft Auto*.

Scotland also manufactures whisky, audio equipment, diesel engines, cars and buses, ships, and aircraft and satellite equipment.

What Scotland Grows, Makes, and Mines

AGRICULTURE (2012)

Barley	1,723,000 metric tons
Potatoes	900,600 metric tons
Wheat	673,300 metric tons

MANUFACTURING (VALUE, 2009)

Electronics	US$3,796,000,000
Textiles	US$697,000,000
Transportation equipment	US$466,000,000

MINING

Oil (2011, all of UK)	1,099,000 barrels a day
Coal (value, 2009)	US$392,000,000

Adam Smith, Economist

Adam Smith is considered the founder of modern economics. Smith was born in Kirkcaldy, Scotland, and studied at the University of Glasgow and Oxford University in England. In his book *The Wealth of Nations*, published in 1776, Smith says that governments should not interfere in the market economy of their nations. He argues that this so-called free market will produce just the right amount of goods and services it requires, "as if guided by an invisible hand."

Agriculture and Forestry

About sixty-five thousand people in Scotland work in agriculture.

About three-quarters of the land in Scotland is used for farming. In the Northwest Highlands and Southern Uplands, sheep farming dominates. Dairy farming and cattle raising occurs

throughout Scotland, but particularly in the southwest. In the east and the Scottish Borders, farms produce barley, potatoes, wheat, and oats. Fruits such as raspberries and strawberries are also grown in the east, mainly near Angus and Tayside.

Roughly 17 percent of Scotland's total land area is forested, and many of these forests are publicly owned. They are managed by the Forestry Commission, which oversees forestlands in England and Scotland. Private landowners, including lumber companies, own the rest of Scotland's forests. The largest tracts of forests are found in Dumfries and Galloway, Argyll, and the Scottish Highlands. In these areas, Scots pine, larch, and Douglas fir are cut down to make lumber and pulp, which is used in the manufacture of paper products.

Scotland's Currency

Scotland uses the same currency as the rest of the United Kingdom, the pound, which uses the symbol £. Each pound is divided into one hundred pence. Some Scottish banks print their own paper money, or banknotes. The Royal Bank of Scotland paper money comes in notes of 1, 5, 10, 20, 50, and 100 pounds. The front side of each note features a portrait of Lord Ilay, one of the founders of the Royal Bank and its first governor. On the back of the notes are images of Scottish castles. For example, the £1 note features Edinburgh Castle and the £5 note shows Culzean Castle. Coins come in amounts of 1, 2, 5, 10, 20, and 50 pence and 1 and 2 pounds. In 2014, £1 equaled US$1.66, and US$1 equaled £0.60.

Fishing

Fishing is an essential part of the Scottish economy. The waters surrounding the country are some of the richest in Europe. The most abundant areas are the North Sea and the seas west of Scotland. The biggest catches are cod, haddock, sole, mackerel, and herring. Other catch includes shellfish such as lobsters, scallops, and crabs.

Aquaculture, or fish farming, is a growing industry along the northwest coast, the Outer Hebrides, and in the northern islands. Some fish, particularly salmon, are raised in cages or pens anchored in bays and inlets of the coasts. Trout are

A fisher hauls prawns up to his boat off the west coast of Scotland. Prawns, which are similar to shrimp, are the second most valuable commercial fishing species in Scotland, after mackerel.

raised in freshwater ponds. Some farms in the Highlands and western and northern islands raise shellfish.

Scotland's fish-processing industry—dealing with fish from the time they are caught until the time they are delivered to the customer—provides more jobs than fishing and aquaculture combined. Aberdeen is the largest fish-processing center in the United Kingdom.

Oil and Gas

Oil and gas fields were discovered in the North Sea in the late 1960s, with the first years of large-scale production coming around 1976. Today, Scotland is one of Europe's largest oil-producing nations, exporting roughly US$51 billion of oil and gas per year worldwide. About 40 percent of Scottish oil and gas is shipped to the rest of the United Kingdom.

Aberdeen is the hub of the oil industry and the inland base of operations for the many offshore oil rigs in the North Sea. The discovery of oil and gas provided a major boost to other cities in the northeast as well. Inverness became home to businesses that manufacture and repair offshore oil platforms. The port city of Leith, just north of Edinburgh, specializes in oil drilling and pipeline equipment. Major oil and gas pipelines run from

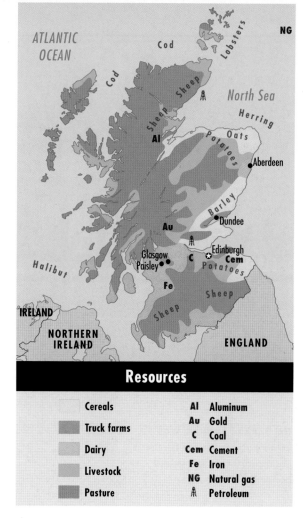

Resources

☐ Cereals	Al Aluminum
▨ Truck farms	Au Gold
▨ Dairy	C Coal
▨ Livestock	Cem Cement
▨ Pasture	Fe Iron
	NG Natural gas
	⚒ Petroleum

The Bank of Scotland was established in the 1600s. Its headquarters is in a grand building in Edinburgh.

the oil fields to terminals in the Orkneys and the Shetlands, where they are transferred to oceangoing tankers. The oil and gas industries provide jobs to about 150,000 workers.

Mining

Scotland has a small mining industry. Much of the mining occurs in the Central Belt. The region includes Britain's largest coalfield as well as large deposits of sand and gravel, clay, silica, and igneous rock. Marble is quarried in the northwest and northeast.

Service Industries

Service industries—businesses that provide services rather than products—are an important part of Scotland's economy, and one of the country's fastest-growing sectors. Scotland is one of Europe's largest financial centers, home to major institutions such as the Bank of Scotland, the Royal Bank of Scotland, Barclays, and Standard Life.

Scotland's tourism industry supports roughly 190,000 jobs and contributes roughly US$7.8 billion annually to the Scottish economy. Each year, about fifteen million people visit Scotland to enjoy the country's natural beauty, historic sites, and cultural institutions. Most tourists come from other parts of the United Kingdom or other parts of Scotland itself. The largest numbers of overseas visitors hail from the United States, France, Germany, Australia, Spain, and Italy.

Other important service industries in Scotland include creative industries such as computer gaming, TV and film, fashion, publishing, and advertising; life sciences, including research; and telecommunications.

Transportation

Scotland has a well-developed system of transportation. The most concentrated network of roads is in the Central Lowlands, where about three-quarters of Scotland's population lives. There are roughly 35,000 miles (56,000 km) of public roads in Scotland, and about 2.7 million licensed vehicles.

ScotRail operates most of the railway services within Scotland as well as services to England. Express trains link major cities. Glasgow and Edinburgh have extensive railway networks that serve their suburban communities. Tourists

Passengers can board ScotRail trains at more than 340 stations around the country.

The World's Most Successful Tea Merchant

Thomas Lipton (1850–1931) was born in Glasgow, the youngest of five children of a working-class family. At age ten, he left school and took a job at a stationery store. Seeking to move up in the world, the youngster quit his job and began working at a shirt-making company. He continued to work at odd jobs and save money until he was able to open a small grocery store in Glasgow in 1870. His business prospered, and by 1888, he had three hundred stores throughout Great Britain.

During this time, tea had become a very popular drink in Great Britain. However, it was too expensive for the average working-class family. Lipton came up with a clever idea. Instead of buying tea from tea growers, he bought tea plantations in Asia and produced his own tea. By controlling the manufacturing process, Lipton was able to sell tea—and lots of it—more cheaply than his competitors. "Lipton Tea" became a household name, and Thomas Lipton became a millionaire. Lipton continued to expand his business in the following decades, buying coffee and cocoa plantations, fruit farms, bakeries, wine stores, and meatpacking companies in the United States. Today, the Lipton brand is still going strong.

enjoy riding Scotland's four rural rail lines, such as the Kyle Line in the Highlands, to take in the scenic countryside.

Aberdeen, Glasgow, and Edinburgh each have airports that accommodate international flights. Edinburgh is the country's largest airport, handling more than nine million passengers each year. Scotland has more than eighty ports. Ferry services carry tourists and freight to Scotland's remote islands off the western coast.

CHAPTER 7

The People of Scotland

IN 2011, THE POPULATION OF SCOTLAND WAS 5,295,400. Eighty-three percent of the total population was born in Scotland, 9 percent in England, 0.7 percent in Northern Ireland, and 0.3 in Wales. The remaining 6 percent or so were born in other countries. Over the years, large numbers of people from Ireland, Poland, Pakistan, India, Bangladesh, China, and Africa have migrated to Scotland.

Opposite: **A couple enjoys a hike in the Scottish Highlands.**

Who Are the Scots?

Most modern-day Scots are descendants of the various tribes that lived in the region in ancient times. Others are more recent arrivals from other parts of the United Kingdom or foreign countries. In the mid-nineteenth century, for example, tens of thousands of Irish came to Scotland to escape starvation when a famine hit Ireland. Between 1841 and 1851, the Irish-born population of Scotland increased by 90 percent. Scotland's

Ethnic Background in Scotland*	
White	96.0%
Asian	2.7%
Black	0.7%
Mixed	0.4%
Other	0.3%

*Total does not equal 100 percent because of rounding.

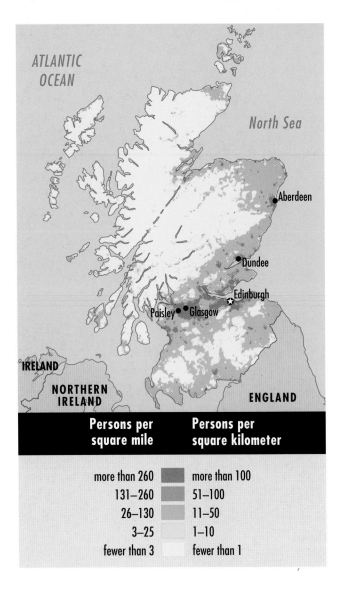

ATLANTIC OCEAN

North Sea

Aberdeen

Dundee

Edinburgh

Paisley • Glasgow

IRELAND

NORTHERN IRELAND

ENGLAND

Persons per square mile	Persons per square kilometer
more than 260	more than 100
131–260	51–100
26–130	11–50
3–25	1–10
fewer than 3	fewer than 1

Population of Major Cities (2011 est.)

Glasgow	589,900
Edinburgh	468,720
Aberdeen	201,680
Dundee	144,170
Paisley	74,570

industrial boom in the nineteenth and early twentieth centuries attracted thousands of workers from northern England. These people found employment in Scotland's factories, mines, and foundries. These days, newcomers are more likely to arrive from Poland and various countries in Asia.

Pakistanis make up the largest minority ethnic group in Scotland today, with about 61,000 living there. About 55,000 Poles reside in Scotland. Chinese are the next largest group, followed by Indians. There are also small numbers of Africans, Caribbean people, and people of Arab descent living in Scotland.

City and Country

About 82 percent of Scottish people live in cities and towns, while about 18 percent live in rural areas. In recent years, some rural areas have experienced an increase in population. From 2001 to 2010, the rural population of Scotland increased by roughly 10 percent, contrasted with only a 1.7 percent increase in the rest of Scotland during that time. Improved job opportunities and more affordable housing in rural areas are the main reasons for the recent migration from cities and towns.

About 70 percent of the country's population lives in the Central Lowlands, the region that includes four of Scotland's five most populous cities—Glasgow, Edinburgh, Dundee, and Paisley. The fifth, Aberdeen, lies on the northeast coast.

Language

English is the dominant language in Scotland, but many languages have been spoken there in the past. The Picts spoke a Celtic language, and Britons in southern Scotland spoke

Scottish scouts read a newspaper while waiting for a flight.

an early form of Welsh. In the ninth century, Viking settlers brought their own language, which evolved into Norn, the dominant language of the Orkney and Shetland Islands until the 1600s.

As Gaelic-speaking Celtic peoples settled throughout the country, Gaelic became the chief language of the land. For centuries, it was the only language spoken by most of Scotland's people, particularly by inhabitants of the Highlands and western regions. By the 1700s, English began to replace Gaelic, especially in the Lowlands. The failure of the Jacobite rebel-

Some parts of Scotland have signs in both English and Gaelic.

English Words with Scottish Gaelic Roots

The English language contains many words that are borrowed from Scottish Gaelic. Here are a few:

English	Scottish Gaelic
clan	clann
galore	gu leor (enough)
glen	gleann (a valley)
pet	peata (tame animal)
slogan	sluagh-ghairm (battle cry)

lions and the government's actions to reduce the influence of Highland culture quickened the decline of Gaelic. When the Education Act of 1872 was enacted, requiring all children to attend schools, English was the language taught in classrooms.

One hundred years ago, roughly 250,000 Scots used Gaelic regularly. Today, about 59,000 people in Scotland speak Gaelic, mainly in the western islands. In recent years, however, there has been a revival of the language and Celtic culture in general. Public schools and universities now offer classes in Gaelic. Government-sponsored television and radio broadcasts are also bringing the language to Scots. In fact, the 2011 census showed a slight increase in the number of young Gaelic speakers.

Scots is another language spoken in Scotland. The language developed from early English. By the eleventh century, it had replaced Gaelic as the dominant language in the Lowlands. Scots grammar is similar to English grammar, and many words are similar, such as *coo* (cow) and *auld* (old). Words we associate with Scotland, such as *lassie*, *laddies*, and *wee*, are Scots.

The Scottish Gaelic Alphabet

Scottish Gaelic is written with eighteen letters. Each letter is named after a tree or a shrub. The thirteen consonants all have more than one pronunciation, depending on their position in a word and which vowels come before or after them. An accent on a vowel indicates a longer version of the vowel.

A   Ailm (elm)
B   Beith (birch)
C   Coll (hazel)
D   Dair (oak)
E   Eadha (aspen)
F   Fearn (alder)
G   Gort (ivy)
H   Uath (hawthorn)
I   Iogh (yew)
L   Luis (rowan)
M   Main (vine)
N   Nain (ash)
O   Oir/Onn (gorse)
P   Peithe (guilder)
R   Ruis (elder)
S   Soil (willow)
T   Teine (furze)
U   Ur (heather)

Common Scottish Gaelic Phrases

Hallo.	Hello.
Dè an t-ainm a tha oirbh?	What's your name?
'S mise . . .	My name is . . .
Ciamar a tha sibh?	How are you?
Tha gu math, tapadh leibh.	I'm well, thank you.
'Se do bheatha.	You're welcome.
Ma 'se ur toil e.	Please.
Slàinte mhòr agad!	Good health to you!
A bheil Gàidhlig agaibh?	Do you speak Gaelic?
Mar sin leat.	Good-bye.

Primary school children usually attend school from about 9:00 a.m. to 3:00 p.m.

Education

Most children in Scotland start primary school at age five. Students attend primary school for seven years. They are then

required to attend secondary schools for four years, until the age of sixteen. At that time, they take a series of national tests in eight subjects called the General Certificate of Secondary Education. After graduation, students may continue their secondary education for two more years. Most students continue their studies or take vocational courses in specialized schools.

Scotland has nineteen universities or other institutions of higher education, which serve about 230,000 students. The oldest is the University of St. Andrews, founded in 1413, and the newest is the University of the Highlands and Islands, established in 2011. All Scottish universities are funded by the Scottish Government and tuition is free for Scottish students. Students can earn undergraduate degrees in four years (called degrees with honors), or in three years (called designated or general degrees).

Students study in a library at the University of Aberdeen, one of three universities in Scotland that was founded prior to the year 1500.

CHAPTER 8

The Faith of a People

CHRISTIANITY IS THE MAIN RELIGION IN SCOTLAND. About 54 percent of the Scottish population considers itself Christian. The Church of Scotland, a Presbyterian faith, is the country's largest church, as well as its official religion. The Church of Scotland is also known as the Kirk, an old Celtic word that means "church."

Today, church membership is in decline. The 2011 census counted slightly more than 1.7 million people who identify themselves as Church of Scotland Presbyterians. That figure represents a decrease of roughly four hundred thousand from ten years earlier.

Opposite: **Saint Giles' Cathedral in Edinburgh is the main cathedral of the Church of Scotland.**

The Arrival of Christianity

Christianity arrived in present-day southern Scotland during the time of the Romans. It was spread through the work of several missionaries, most notably Saint Columba, who established a monastery on the island of Iona in the Inner Hebrides. Saint Columba and his followers worked among the Gaels in the west, as well as among the Picts in the north and east and the Anglos in what is present-day England. In the centuries that followed, religious centers became important seats of education and political influence.

Saint Columba, a monk from Ireland, arrived on the island of Iona in Scotland in 563. He and twelve followers built a church there and spread Christianity throughout Scotland.

Little is known about the life of Saint Andrew, Scotland's patron saint, but it is believed he was a fisherman on the Sea of Galilee in what is now Israel. During the early first century, Andrew became a follower of Jesus. Andrew preached Christianity in Europe and central Asia, converting many subjects of the Roman Empire to the new religion. Angered by Andrew's actions, Roman officials ordered him to be executed. It is said that he was crucified on the Greek island of Patras. Legend holds that in the mid-eighth century a holy man named Regulus was told in a dream to dig up Andrew's bones and take them to the west by ship. He was to rebury the bones and establish a church on the site of the new grave. After a difficult journey, Regulus managed to reach Scotland's east coast, where he founded a church and the town of St. Andrews.

Protestantism in Scotland

By the 1500s, religious conflict had developed between Roman Catholics and Protestants. Protestant reformers soon broke away from the Roman Catholic Church. In 1560, Protestant reformers led by John Knox abolished the authority of the pope and established their own church. More than one hundred years of religious strife followed as the new church was split on whether to use a Presbyterian or an Episcopalian form of government. Presbyterians favored a church free from state control and a leadership without bishops. The conflict ended in 1689 when Scottish lawmakers declared the Church of Scotland would adopt a Presbyterian government.

Religion in Scotland (2011)	
No religion	36.7%
Church of Scotland	32.4%
Roman Catholic Church	15.9%
Did not answer	7.0%
Other Christian	5.5%
Islam	1.4%
Hinduism	0.3%
Other religions	0.3%
Buddhism	0.2%
Sikhism	0.2%
Judaism	0.1%

In 1843, members of
the Free Church of
Scotland signed papers
separating from the
Church of Scotland.

In the early eighteenth century, divisions arose within the Church of Scotland. The Moderates were interested mainly in social and cultural matters. The Evangelicals were more concerned with spreading their religion through preaching. In 1843, the Evangelicals broke away from the Church of Scotland and formed the Free Church of Scotland. Many of the Church of Scotland's foremost scholars and missionaries joined the Free Church.

Over the years, the two churches grew closer again, and in 1929 they recombined. Some people, however, opposed rejoining the Church of Scotland, and a small Free Church of Scotland still exists. Today, the Free Church is especially strong on some of the islands of the Outer Hebrides. It has about one hundred congregations throughout the country, with a membership of around 12,500 people.

Roman Catholicism

Roman Catholicism is the second-largest religion in the country. About 16 percent of Scotland's population describe themselves as Roman Catholic. Many Roman Catholics in the country are descendants of Irish immigrants who came to Scotland from Ireland. There was a large wave of Irish immigrants beginning with the Irish potato famine in the 1840s. Another wave of Irish immigrants arrived during the 1920s to the 1940s to work in Scotland's factories. The two most Catholic areas of Scotland are the southern islands of the Hebrides, such as Barra and South Uist, and the eastern suburbs of Glasgow. The people in the Hebrides are long-standing Scottish Catholics who did not convert to Protestantism at the time of the Reformation. Those near Glasgow are mainly of Irish descent.

Catholic priests lead a mass at St. Mary's Cathedral in Edinburgh.

Children release balloons in front of the Edinburgh Central Mosque. The first Muslims arrived in Scotland in the late eighteenth century, but most Muslims in Scotland today are from families who immigrated in the twentieth century.

Other Religions

Scottish law guarantees freedom of religion. Muslims, Hindus, Buddhists, Sikhs, Jews, and small numbers of people of other faiths also live in Scotland. Muslims, who practice the religion of Islam, are the fastest-growing religious group in Scotland. In 2011, roughly eighty thousand Muslims lived in Scotland,

Important Religious Holidays

Holy Thursday	March–April
Good Friday	March–April
Easter	March–April
Pentecost	May–June
Christmas	December 25

nearly twice the number from ten years earlier. The Sikh community in Scotland is centered in Glasgow and Edinburgh. Most Sikhs in Scotland come from families who emigrated from India during the late twentieth century. Scotland's modern Jewish community dates back to emigrants from Holland and Belgium who settled in Edinburgh in the eighteenth century. Scotland's Jewish population peaked at about eighty thousand in the mid-twentieth century and declined after World War II, as many Jews moved to the United States or Israel. Today, there are roughly six thousand Jews living in Scotland.

Scottish Mythology

Scotland has a long and rich history of myths, folklore, and legends. Many myths come from the Hebrides off the western coast. Surrounded by sea, these isolated and mostly uninhabited islands have inspired abundant tales of enchantment and mysterious creatures.

One bizarre mythical creature of Scottish folklore is the kelpie (below), a strong and powerful water horse said to live in the rivers and lochs of Scotland. Its smooth, white skin is cold to the touch. Kelpies are said to lure humans into the water to drown them. According to the story, the kelpie convinces a person to ride on its back. Once its victim agrees, the horse's skin becomes like glue, trapping the unlucky person. The kelpie then swims to the bottom of the river, drowning and then eating its prey. It is said that kelpies can also appear on land in a shaggy human form.

Another legend surrounds the Blue Men of the Minch. They are said to live in the waters around the Isle of Lewis off Scotland's northwestern coast. These blue-skinned merman-like creatures live deep in underwater caves. It is said they sometimes swim to the water's surface and try to overturn passing ships. But there is a catch: the captain of a boat could save his ship and crew by telling the Blue Men a clever riddle.

CHAPTER 9

A Creative Culture

DESPITE ITS RELATIVELY SMALL SIZE AND population, Scotland has contributed much to world culture. With a long heritage of storytelling and a national commitment to education, Scots have produced impressive bodies of work in literature, music, art, architecture, and film.

Literary Giants

Duncan Ban Macintyre (1724–1812) is one of Scotland's most beloved poets. Macintyre worked for a time as a gamekeeper in the Highlands, and he often wrote lovingly about the Scottish wilds. In a poem called "In Praise of Ben Dorain," he praised the beauty of a hill named Ben Dorain. It begins,

> *Honor past all bens*
> *to Ben Dorain.*
> *Of all beneath the sun*
> *I adore her.*

class Scots. Gavin Hamilton (1723–1798) and Alexander Runciman (1736–1785) painted scenes of ancient Rome. The late nineteenth century saw a revival in Celtic culture. The movement was dominated by the work of the Glasgow Boys, a group of painters that focused on realistic subjects, such as rural

In 2011, J. K. Rowling attended the premier of the eighth and final *Harry Potter* film. The movies were based on her novels, which have sold about 450 million copies worldwide.

and street scenes. The leaders of the movement included Joseph Crawhall, George Henry, and James Guthrie. A later group of artists known as the Spook School included architect and artist Charles Rennie Mackintosh (1868–1928) and his wife, glass artist Margaret Macdonald. Their work blended elements of Celtic revival art and those of Japanese art and culture.

More recent Scottish artists include Joan Eardley, who illustrated street life in mid-twentieth-century Glasgow. Her subjects include children playing in the streets and scenes of the shipyards at the port of Glasgow. Robert MacBryde was a contemporary still-life painter and theater set designer.

Joan Eardley was renowned for her sympathetic paintings of Glasgow children.

Scotland's Castles

It has been estimated that there were once about three thousand castles in Scotland. Today, dozens of castles and fortresses still dot the countryside. Some are in ruins, but others remain in near-perfect condition. Here are a few:

Edinburgh Castle is Scotland's most famous castle. Its oldest part, St. Margaret's Chapel, dates from the twelfth century. The castle houses the Crown Jewels of Scotland and the Stone of Destiny.

Stirling Castle (below), located in Stirling, was the site of numerous battles during the Scottish wars of independence. In 1746, Bonnie Prince Charlie unsuccessfully tried to capture the castle. Mary, Queen of Scots was crowned here in 1542.

Eilean Donan Castle (above) sits on a tiny island in Loch Duich in the western Highlands. The castle was built in the early thirteenth century as a defense against Viking raiders. Eilean Donan was demolished by British troops after the failure of the Jacobite rebellion in 1719, but has been completely restored, and today is a favorite tourist destination.

Near Aberdeen, Dunnottar Castle stands high atop massive rocky cliffs, surrounded on three sides by the North Sea. William Wallace captured the castle from the English in 1297. The Scottish crown jewels were hidden in the castle in the seventeenth century. In 1715, the castle's owner, a Jacobite named George Keith, fled after the failure of the rebellion, and the British government seized the castle.

Music

Many people associate Scottish music with the slow, haunting melodies of bagpipes. But there's a lot more to the Scottish music scene than that. Today's pop and rock bands owe thanks to the Clouds, an Edinburgh-based progressive rock band that earned a small but loyal following throughout Great Britain. In the 1970s, bands such as Nazareth and the Sensational Alex Harvey Band gained international fame. The most commercially successful Scottish pop band of the 1970s was the Bay City Rollers, who sold more than seventy million records worldwide. In the 1980s, artists such as Annie Lennox of the Eurythmics, Big Country, Simple Minds, and the Cocteau Twins were major rock acts. In the 1990s, Belle and Sebastian emerged from Glasgow to become one of the most influential and best loved indie rock bands. A recent trend to blend traditional

The Cocteau Twins were at the peak of their popularity in the late 1980s and early 1990s. They were known for their atmospheric music.

The Bagpipes

Contrary to common belief, the bagpipes are not exclusively a Scottish instrument. Bagpipes have been played for centuries throughout Europe, India, Russia, and parts of the Middle East and North Africa. Bagpipes first appeared in Scotland before 1400. The Scottish Highland bagpipe is the most common type of bagpipe played in Scotland. The instrument consists of an inflatable bag, a blowpipe, three drone pipes, and a chanter. The bag is held under the arm. The player inflates the bag by blowing into the blowpipe. Pressure from the arm on the bag controls the flow of air to the chanter and three drone pipes. The piper plays the melodies on the chanter, which has finger holes, similar to a recorder. Only nine notes can be played on Highland bagpipe.

Despite its limited range, the Scottish Highland bagpipe produces a very large and powerful sound that can travel long distances. For this reason, Scottish armies used bagpipes to summon troops and give signals in combat.

Celtic music with rock and jazz has produced acts such as Shooglenifty and Peatbog Faeries.

Scotland has produced several notable classical music composers, including Ronald Stevenson, Thea Musgrave, and William Sweeney. Craig Armstrong has composed award-winning music for motion pictures. Lovers of classical music enjoy performances by the Royal Scottish National Orchestra, the Scottish Chamber Orchestra, and Scottish Opera.

Through the ages, Scottish folk music took different forms in different regions of the country. Folk music in the Lowlands and Scottish Borders is more similar to English folk music. The songs are usually sung in English or Scots, including the songs of Robert Burns. Singer Jean Redpath, a huge fan of American folk music of the 1960s, is known for her interpretations of Burns's songs and other traditional Scottish music. The music in the Highlands and Hebrides is Gaelic. Songs are often sung unaccompanied by music in a style called *puirt à beul*, meaning "tunes from a mouth." When music is played, the instruments of choice are the Highland bagpipes, fiddle, and harp. In the Shetland and Orkney Islands, fiddle playing is most common.

Each year, Scotland hosts major music festivals that draw attendees from around the world. The Edinburgh International Festival held in August lasts three weeks and features world-class performers in classical, rock, folk, and jazz music, and

The Royal Scottish National Orchestra and the Edinburgh Festival Chorus take a bow in 2013.

opera, dance, and theater. The festival is held around the same time as the larger Edinburgh Fringe, the world's largest arts festival. Each year, musicians and artists from dozens of countries perform or display their art in more than 250 different venues, or performing spaces. The Callander Jazz and Blues Festival is held each fall, offering a star-studded lineup of local and international performers. RockNess, held on the banks of Loch Ness, has featured major artists such as Fatboy Slim, the English folk band Mumford & Sons, and the American psychedelic rock band the Flaming Lips. The festival has been called "the only festival with its own monster" because of its scenic location at the home of Nessie, the Loch Ness Monster.

Fans cheer for Mumford & Sons at the RockNess Festival in 2012.

Film and Television

Scotland has been the birthplace of many successful actors. Sean Connery is probably best known for playing the suave secret agent James Bond. Connery portrayed Bond in seven films. Deborah Kerr was one of the top actresses of the mid-twentieth century. Known for her grace and versatility, she was nominated for six Academy Awards, including for her roles in *From Here to Eternity* and *The King and I*. More recent Scottish actors who have gained international fame include Ewan McGregor, who played the young Obi-Wan Kenobi in the *Star Wars* movies; David Tennant, who made a name for himself as TV's *Dr. Who*; and James McAvoy, who appeared in *X-Men: First Class*.

The Rangers (in blue) and the Celtic are both based in Glasgow. Both teams were founded in the 1800s.

Sports

Scotland's most popular sport is soccer, called football in much of the world. It is played in the streets and schoolyards and in huge stadiums filled with thousands of spectators. The Scottish Professional Football League is the country's professional soccer organization. Forty-two clubs belong to the league, representing all regions of Scotland. Scotland's two most successful teams over the years have been the Rangers and the Celtic of Glasgow. The Rangers have won more league championships than any other soccer team in the world.

Scotland is the birthplace of golf. The first recorded mention of golf dates back to 1457, when the king banned the sport because young men were playing too much golf instead of taking part in activities useful for military training. There are more than five hundred golf courses spread throughout Scotland, including some of the world's finest. The Royal and Ancient Golf Club of St. Andrews in the Lowlands is Scotland's oldest and most honored course. Many golf terms have their origin in the Scottish Lowlands, such as *caddie*, *par*, *tee*, and *birdie*.

Rugby is played throughout Scotland. Cycling is a popular sport, and Scotland has produced several world-class cyclists. Edinburgh-born Sir Chris Hoy has won six gold medals and one silver medal in cycling events in the Olympic Games.

The winter game of curling originated in Scotland about three hundred years ago. In this game, players slide stones across ice, trying to get nearest to a target. The Scottish men's team is the most successful in the world, having won thirty-two world championships. Water polo is believed to have originated in Scotland in the late nineteenth century. After a decline in popularity during the 1990s, water polo is coming back strong with increasing numbers of new clubs and competitions.

The Highland Games are amazing and unique athletic competitions held in Scotland as a way of celebrating Celtic culture. The largest Highland Games are held every August in Cowal, where more than 3,500 competitors and nearly 23,000 spectators gather. A feature of the games is tossing the caber, a tree trunk about 20 feet (6 m) long and weighing 175 pounds (79 kg). The aim is to toss the caber so that it turns end over end in the air, falling away from the tosser. Another popular event is the sheaf toss. In this event, athletes must lift a 20-pound (9 kg) bundle of straw with a pitchfork and toss it over a raised bar. Highland Games also feature bagpipe bands, Celtic folk bands, and dance.

CHAPTER 10

Daily Life

IF YOU ASKED THE MILLIONS OF VISITORS WHO TRAVEL to Scotland every year why they go, the answer you're likely to get is, the people. Scots are friendly, warm, and welcoming. They are proud of their culture and its long traditions.

Opposite: **Pedestrians crowd a major shopping street in Glasgow.**

Food

Traditional Scottish cuisine is a blend of homegrown foods and recipes mixed with British and European influences. Fish, game animals, dairy, and fresh fruits and vegetables are the main ingredients in Scottish cooking. In recent years, the influx of immigrants from abroad has introduced Chinese, Indian, Japanese, Polish, and Mexican cuisines to Scottish diners.

Yum or Yuck?

Haggis might sound unappealing to most non-Scots, but it's Scotland's national dish. It was a favorite of poet Robert Burns, who described it as "a glorious sight, warm-reekin, rich." Haggis is made by chopping up a sheep's organs (heart, liver, windpipe, and lungs), mixing them with beef fat, and allowing it all to soak overnight. Oatmeal, onions, spices, and gravy are added, and the entire mixture is stuffed into a sheep's stomach and boiled for a few hours. It is served hot with *bashed neeps*, or mashed turnips, and *chappit tatties*, or mashed potatoes. The dish is especially popular on Burns Night, held every January 25 to celebrate the poet's birthday. In fact, many Scots eat haggis only at Burns Night suppers, because they consider it a patriotic obligation.

Fish and chips has long been a standard quick meal in Scotland. The fish are covered in batter and then deep fried. These pieces of fish are served with french fries, which are called "chips" throughout the United Kingdom.

The "full" Scottish breakfast includes fried eggs, bacon, link sausage or lorne sausage (a square patty), fried tomatoes or onions, baked beans, and black pudding, a type of sausage made with cooked animal blood. Arbroath smokies, named for their place of origin, Arbroath, on the North Sea coast, are a type of smoked haddock. They are often served with a poached egg on top. Butteries might also be served after the main hot dish. Also known as Aberdeen rolls, these round and soft bread specialties are served warm with butter. Oatcakes made with oatmeal and bacon fat, Scottish oatmeal, and porridge are other popular breakfast choices in Scotland.

Traditional Scottish dishes cover a wide range of tasty foods, from hearty soups, to fish, seafood, poultry, and meat, to delicious vegetables, to sweet desserts and moist, tender cakes.

Cullen skink is a thick soup make with smoked haddock, potatoes, and onions. It is often served as the first course at formal Scottish dinners. The soup originated in the town of Cullen, on the northeast coast. Partan bree is a soup made with crab, rice, and milk. Its name comes from the Gaelic word *partan* (crab) and the Scots word *bree* (soup).

Cullen skink is a hearty soup, popular throughout Scotland.

Rollmops are pickled herring fillets wrapped around a filling of onions, pickles, or olives. Collops is a meat dish of thinly sliced or ground beef, lamb, or deer. The meat is mixed with onions, beef fat, and salt and pepper, and baked or roasted. It is traditionally served with toast and mashed potatoes. Stovies are dishes meant to use leftover food. Potatoes, onions, carrots, or other vegetables are cooked with gravy and seasonings, and then a meat, such as roast beef or corned beef, is added. Stovies are usually served with oatcakes.

Rollmops are often served with slices of scallion or onion.

Cock-a-Leekie Soup

Though cock-a-leekie soup is considered Scotland's national soup, it probably originated in France. This hearty dish is a favorite on cold winter days, making either a simple dinner or a wholesome lunch. Have an adult help you with this recipe.

Ingredients

1 tablespoon oil

1¼ pounds skinless chicken thighs

1¼ pounds skinless chicken breast halves

Four 14½-ounce cans chicken broth

2 cups water

2 large celery stalks, halved crosswise

1 large carrot, peeled

2 large garlic cloves, peeled

6 leeks, white and light-green parts only, halved lengthwise, thinly sliced crosswise

12 pitted prunes, quartered (⅔ cup packed)

½ cup barley

½ cup finely chopped fresh parsley

Directions

1. Heat the oil in a large pot over medium heat. Add the chicken thighs and cook until browned, about 8 minutes. Remove the thighs and put them in a bowl. Then brown the chicken breasts and put them in the bowl.

2. Add the chicken broth, water, celery, carrot, and garlic to the pot. Bring this mixture to a boil. Add the chicken. Reduce the heat and simmer for 1 hour. Remove the chicken and put it on a plate. Remove the vegetables and put them on a separate plate.

3. Add the leeks, prunes, and barley to the broth. Bring this mixture to a boil, reduce the heat, and simmer for about 40 minutes, until it thickens.

4. When the chicken has cooled, shred the meat. Dice the carrots and celery after they cool. Stir the chicken, carrot, celery, and parsley into the soup. Heat the soup until all the ingredients are warm, and then serve.

The top of a Dundee cake is usually decorated with almonds.

Clapshot is a favorite vegetable dish served with haggis, oatcakes, or sausage. It is a mixture of mashed turnips, potatoes, chives, and butter. Rumbledethumps is a traditional dish from the Scottish Borders. It is made by sautéing onion and cabbage in butter and adding potatoes mashed with butter. The mixture is topped with cheese and baked. It can be served with a main dish or eaten as a main dish itself.

Dundee cake is a popular dessert. The cake is made with fruits such as raisins, or currants, and almonds. Black bun is a fruitcake completely wrapped in pastry. The fruitcake mixture includes raisins, almonds, ginger, currants, cinnamon, pepper, and other flavorings. It is a favorite during Hogmanay, the Scottish New Year's celebration.

Festivals and Celebrations

Hogmanay is the name for the Scottish New Year's celebration. The most popular custom on this festive day is called first footing. This refers to the first person to step across the threshold of a friend's or neighbor's house. The person must be male, and he must bring gifts, such as coal for the fire or bread or cakes to feed the family. The first-footer is believed to bring good luck for the rest of the year.

Some regions of Scotland have developed their own Hogmanay customs. In Stonehaven, in northeast Scotland,

People carry torches through the streets of Edinburgh to celebrate Hogmanay.

National Holidays

New Year's Day	January 1
New Year Holiday	January 2
Good Friday	March or April
May Day	First Monday in May
Spring Holiday	Last Monday in May
Summer Holiday	First Monday in August
St. Andrews Day	November 30
Christmas	December 25
Boxing Day	December 26

residents make balls of wire and fill them with old newspaper, rags, and sticks. The balls are attached to wire or chain ropes. As the town house bells are rung to announce the New Year, the balls are set on fire. Swinging the burning balls around their heads, the participants march through the town, often accompanied by pipers, drummers, and fireworks displays.

Whuppity Scoorie is celebrated by people in Lanark on March 1 to mark the coming of spring. It's believed that the name Whuppity Scoorie comes from an evil fairylike creature in a Scottish fairy tale. When the local bells are rung at 6:00 p.m., children walk around the church in a clockwise direction swinging paper balls around their heads. After three laps, adults throw handfuls of coins and the children scurry to catch them. No one is certain how this custom arose.

Samhain is a festival held from October 31 to November 1, marking the end of summer and the beginning of winter. Ancient tradition claimed that during this time spirits of the dead were able to enter the world of living humans. To welcome the spirits and win their favor for the coming winter,

Earth Laid Upon a Corpse

One traditional burial custom that originated in the Highlands is still practiced today. A wooden plate is placed on the chest of the deceased and piled with dirt and salt. This custom is called "earth laid upon a corpse" and is said to represent the person's future in the afterlife. The dirt represents the person's physical body. Because salt is used as a preservative, it symbolizes the person's soul, because a soul does not decay or die.

people offered food, sacrificed animals, and lit bonfires. People often went from house to house, singing or reciting poetry, and wearing costumes and masks to please the spirits. Many of these ancient Samhain customs are still practiced.

People join a Halloween procession in Edinburgh. Samhain was an important influence on the development of Halloween.

Traditional Highland Dress

Scots today dress just the same as people do in the United States and Canada. Jeans and T-shirts are the standard clothes of young people. But for special occasions, many Scots look to the past.

Traditional Highland clothing has had a huge revival in recent years, and it's common to see it on the streets of Highland towns and at formal occasions throughout the country. Highland dress originated with the garment called

Scottish men sometimes wear traditional Highland clothing on special occasions.

the *feileadh mor*, or great plaid, or *breacan feile*, or belted plaid. This was a long piece of wool wrapped around the waist and held in place with a belt. The rest of it was worn over the shoulder and secured with a brooch. The great plaid evolved into the philabeg, the kilt commonly associated with modern Highland dress. It is made from long pieces of wool folded into many pleats. Only men wear the kilt. The look is topped off with black or brown shoes, long woolen stockings, and a jacket over a dress shirt. A sporran, or leather purse, is worn in front of the kilt. It serves as a pocket on the pocketless kilt. A *sgian dubh*, a small, single-edged knife is tucked into the top of the stocking, worn on either leg. Traditionally, the knife was used for eating and cutting food, as well as for protection. A dirk, or dagger, is worn at the side. The tartan patterns woven into kilts are called setts.

Looking to the Future

Throughout the centuries, Scots have faced years of hardship and political and social strife. Despite their difficulties, the Scots have never abandoned their heritage or surrendered their sense of pride. Today, they face an uncertain future—a young Parliament, devolution, and the possibility of complete independence—with hope and optimism. In the words of Robert Burns:

> *O Scotia! my dear, my native soil!*
> *For whom my warmest wish to Heaven is sent*
> *Long may thy hardy sons of rustic toil*
> *Be blest with health, peace, and sweet content!*

Timeline

SCOTTISH HISTORY		WORLD HISTORY	
Hunter-gatherers arrive in Scotland from the European mainland.	ca. 8000 BCE		
		ca. 2500 BCE — The Egyptians build the pyramids and the Sphinx in Giza.	
People begin working bronze in Scotland.	ca. 1800 BCE	ca. 563 BCE — The Buddha is born in India.	
Celts begin settling in Scotland.	ca. 500 BCE		
The Romans invade Scotland.	43 CE		
Romans build Hadrian's Wall to defend against peoples in what is now Scotland.	120s		
Scots, from Ireland, settle on Scotland's west coast.	400s	313 CE — The Roman emperor Constantine legalizes Christianity.	
Anglo-Saxon tribes begin invading the British Isles.	ca. 450		
Saint Columba begins converting people to Christianity.	563		
Vikings from Norway begin establishing settlements.	700s	610 — The Prophet Muhammad begins preaching a new religion called Islam.	
Kenneth MacAlpin unites the Scots and Picts, becoming the first king of Scotland.	843		
		1054 — The Eastern (Orthodox) and Western (Roman Catholic) Churches break apart.	
		1095 — The Crusades begin.	
English forces take the Scottish Stone of Destiny back to England.	1296	1215 — King John seals the Magna Carta.	
		1300s — The Renaissance begins in Italy.	
Scots defeat the English at the Battle of Bannockburn, establishing Scottish independence.	1314	1347 — The plague sweeps through Europe.	
		1453 — Ottoman Turks capture Constantinople, conquering the Byzantine Empire.	
		1492 — Columbus arrives in North America.	

SCOTTISH HISTORY

The English defeat the Scots.	**1513**
The Presbyterian Church becomes the national Church of Scotland.	**1560**
James VI of Scotland becomes King James I of England.	**1603**
The Treaty of Union unites Scotland, England, and Wales to form Great Britain.	**1707**
Jacobite rebels are defeated at the Battle of Sheriffmuir.	**1715**
Prince Charles Edward Stuart leads the second Jacobite rebellion; Jacobites are defeated at the Battle of Culloden.	**1746**
The Education Act for Scotland is signed, requiring most children ages six to fifteen to attend school.	**1872**
The Scottish National Party is founded; it calls for separation from the United Kingdom.	**1934**
Oil is discovered in the North Sea.	**1969**
A Scottish Parliament is reinstated.	**1999**
Opinion polls show that a majority of Scots oppose independence.	**2013**

WORLD HISTORY

1500s	Reformers break away from the Catholic Church, and Protestantism is born.
1776	The U.S. Declaration of Independence is signed.
1789	The French Revolution begins.
1865	The American Civil War ends.
1879	The first practical lightbulb is invented.
1914	World War I begins.
1917	The Bolshevik Revolution brings communism to Russia.
1929	A worldwide economic depression begins.
1939	World War II begins.
1945	World War II ends.
1969	Humans land on the Moon.
1975	The Vietnam War ends.
1989	The Berlin Wall is torn down as communism crumbles in Eastern Europe.
1991	The Soviet Union breaks into separate states.
2001	Terrorists attack the World Trade Center in New York City and the Pentagon near Washington, D.C.
2004	A tsunami in the Indian Ocean destroys coastlines in Africa, India, and Southeast Asia.
2008	The United States elects its first African American president.

Fast Facts

Official name: Scotland

Capital: Edinburgh

Official languages: English, Scottish Gaelic

Edinburgh

Scotland

SCOTLAND

- • Cities of more than 75,000 people
- ○ Other cities
- ⬡ National capital
- ∴ Archaeological site

0   50 miles

0   50 kilometers

Scottish flag

National church:	Church of Scotland (Presbyterian)
National anthem:	"Flower of Scotland" (unofficial)
Type of government:	Constitutional monarchy
Head of state:	British monarch
Head of government:	First minister
Area of country:	30,414 square miles (78,772 sq km)
Latitude and longitude of geographic center:	57°00' N, 4°00' W
Bordering countries and waters:	Atlantic Ocean to the north and west; North Sea to the east: England to the south
Highest elevation:	Ben Nevis, 4,409 feet (1,344 meters)
Lowest elevation:	Sea level, along the coast
Average high temperature:	In Edinburgh, 45°F (7°C) in January, 66°F (19°C) in July
Average low temperature:	In Edinburgh, 35°F (2°C) in January, 53°F (12°C) in July
Average annual precipitation:	28 inches (71 cm) in Edinburgh

Cape Wrath

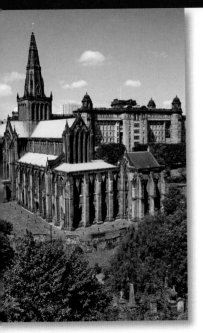

Glasgow Cathedral

National population (2011):	5,295,400	
Population of major cities (2011 est.):	Glasgow	589,900
	Edinburgh	468,720
	Aberdeen	201,680
	Dundee	144,170
	Paisley	74,570

Landmarks:
- ▶ *Edinburgh Castle*, Edinburgh
- ▶ *Glasgow Cathedral*, Glasgow
- ▶ *Loch Ness*, Inverness
- ▶ *National Museum of Scotland*, Edinburgh
- ▶ *Skara Brae*, Mainland, Orkney Islands

Currency

Economy: Manufacturing plays a large role in Scotland's economy. Major products include textiles, electronics, office machinery, vehicles and aircraft, steel, and metal. Since the discovery of oil under the North Sea in 1969, the oil industry has been central to the Scottish economy. Services such as tourism and finance have also been growing. Large numbers of cattle and sheep are raised in Scotland, and fisheries bring in large hauls of herring and cod. Major crops include barley, potatoes, wheat, and oats.

Currency: British pound (£); in 2014, £1 equaled US$1.66, and US$1 equaled £0.60

System of weights and measures: Metric system and imperial units

Literacy rate (2005 est.): 99%

College student

J. K. Rowling

Common Scottish Gaelic words and phrases:

Ciamar a tha sibh?	How are you?
Tha gu math, tapadh leibh.	I'm well, thank you.
'Se do bheatha.	You're welcome.
Ma 'se ur toil e.	Please.
Slàinte mhòr agad!	Good health to you!
Tha mi duilich.	I'm sorry.
Ceart gu leòr.	Okay.
Gabhaibh mo leisgeul.	Excuse me.
Dè an t-ainm a tha oirbh?	What's your name?
'S mise . . .	My name is . . .

Prominent Scots:

Alexander Graham Bell (1847–1922)
Inventor

Robert Burns (1759–1796)
Poet

Arthur Conan Doyle (1859–1930)
Author

Chris Hoy (1976–)
Cyclist

Charles Rennie Mackintosh (1868–1928)
Architect and designer

Mary I (Mary, Queen of Scots) (1542–1587)
Queen

J. K. Rowling (1965–)
Author

Adam Smith (1723–1790)
Philosopher and economist

James Watt (1736–1819)
Engineer

To Find Out More

Books

▶ Levy, Patricia, and Jacqueline Ong. *Scotland*. New York: Marshall Cavendish, 2011.

▶ McNee, Ian. *Kings and Queens*. Witney, Oxfordshire, England, UK: Usborne Books, 2012.

▶ Steele, Philip. *The Celts*. London, England: Wayland Publishers, 2011.

▶ Wilson, Barbara Ker. *Stories from Scotland*. Oxford, England: Oxford University Press, 2009.

DVDs

▶ *A History of Scotland*. BBC Home Entertainment, 2010.

▶ *Scotland Highlands*. BFS Entertainment, 2012.

▶ *Scotland Revealed*. BFS Entertainment, 2010.

▶ *Visions of Scotland*. Acorn Media, 2007.

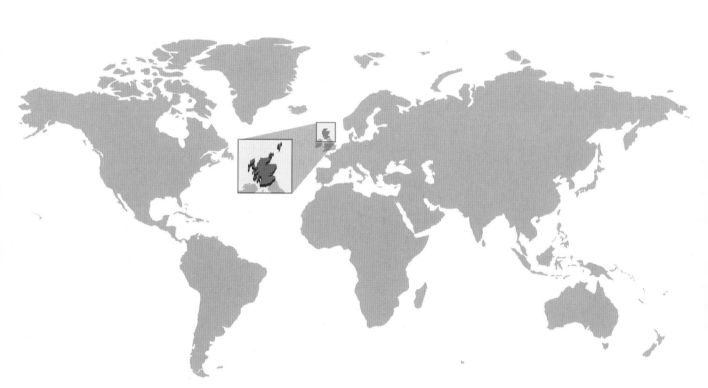

▶ Visit this Scholastic Web site for more information on Scotland:
www.factsfornow.scholastic.com
Enter the keyword **Scotland**

Index

Page numbers in *italics* indicate illustrations.

Meet the Author

NEL YOMTOV IS AN AWARD-WINNING AUTHOR and editor with a passion for writing nonfiction books for young people. In recent years, he has written books about history and geography as well as graphic-novel adaptations of classic mythology, sports biographies, and science topics.

Yomtov was born in New York City. After graduating college, he worked at Marvel Comics, where he handled all phases of comic book production work. Yomtov has also written, edited, and colored hundreds of Marvel comic books. He has served as editorial director of a children's nonfiction book publisher and also as publisher of the Hammond World Atlas book division. In between, he squeezed in a two-year stint as consultant to Major League Baseball, where he helped supervise an educational program for elementary and middle schools throughout the country.

Yomtov lives in the New York area with his wife, Nancy, a teacher and writer, and son, Jess, a sports journalist.

Photo Credits

Photographs ©: cover: VisitBritain/Britain on View/Getty Images; back cover: VisitBritain/Britain on View/Getty Images; 2: Rieger Bertrand/Hemis.fr/Superstock, Inc.; 5: Rick Gerharter/Getty Images; 6 left: Colin McPherson/Corbis Images; 6 center: VisitBritain/Andy Sewell/Getty Images; 6 right: Ivan Vdovin/age fotostock/Superstock, Inc.; 7 left: Jeff J Mitchell/Getty Images; 7 right: age fotostock/Superstock, Inc.; 8: FLPA/Superstock, Inc.; 10: The Granger Collection, New York; 12: David Moir/Reuters/Landov; 13: Martin M303/Shutterstock, Inc.; 14: Derek Croucher/Alamy Images; 16: Kathleen Norris Cook/Alamy Images; 17: Robert Harding Picture Library/Superstock, Inc.; 18: Robert Harding Picture Library/Superstock, Inc.; 20: SMC Image Archive; 21: Jennifer Thompson/Corbis Images; 22: Robert Harding Picture Library/Superstock, Inc.; 23: International Photobank/Alamy Images; 25: Blackout Concepts/Alamy Images; 26: Andrew Hopkins/Alamy Images; 27 left: Scottish Viewpoint/Alamy Images; 27 right: Heartland Arts/Shutterstock, Inc.; 28: age fotostock/Superstock, Inc.; 30: Doug Houghton/Alamy Images; 31: Les Gibbon/Alamy Images; 32: Targn Pleiades/Shutterstock, Inc.; 33: Mark Caunt/Shutterstock, Inc.; 34: John Peter Photography/Alamy Images; 35: Science Photo Library/Alamy Images; 36 top: ColorWorld/Shutterstock, Inc.; 36 bottom: Photononstop/Superstock, Inc.; 37: David\"hajes\"Hajek/Dreamstime; 38: Ainars Aunins/Shutterstock, Inc.; 39: Pukhov Konstantin/Shutterstock, Inc.; 40: nagelestock.com/Alamy Images; 42: Lebrecht Music and Arts Photo Library/Alamy Images; 43: Robert Fishman/age fotostock; 45: Robert Estall photo agency/Alamy Images; 46: Chronicle/Alamy Images; 47: Image Asset Management Ltd./Superstock, Inc.; 48: Mary Evans Picture Library/Alamy Images; 49: Chris Bacon/AP Images; 50: Ken Crocket/Alamy Images; 51: Look and Learn/Bridgeman Art Library; 53: Iberfoto/Superstock, Inc.; 54: Chronicle/Alamy Images; 55: John A Cameron/Shutterstock, Inc.; 56: GL Archive/Alamy Images; 57: Image Asset Management Ltd./Alamy Images; 58: Album/Prisma/Superstock, Inc.; 59: Hulton-Deutsch Collection/Corbis Images; 60: Mary Evans Picture Library/The Image Works; 61: DEA/A. Dagli Orti/Getty Images; 62: Pictorial Press Ltd./Alamy Images; 63: David Cheskin/AP Images; 64: Andrew Milligan/AP Images; 67: Bloomberg/Getty Images; 68 left: Jeff Overs/Getty Images; 68 right: Lawrence Jackson/AP Images; 69: Ken Jack/Demotix/Corbis Images; 70: wavebreakmedia/Shutterstock, Inc.; 71: Jeff J Mitchell/Getty Images; 72: Press Association/AP Images; 73: Ivan Vdovin/age fotostock/Superstock, Inc.; 74: Dennis Hardley/Alamy Images; 76: Michael Doolittle/Alamy Images; 78 top: SKFStock/Alamy Images; 78 bottom: David Gowans/Alamy Images; 79: Stockcube/Dreamstime; 80: Colin McPherson/Corbis Images; 82: imagebroker.net/Superstock, Inc.; 83: Dennis K. Johnson/Getty Images; 84: Steve Lindridge/Alamy Images; 85: The Art Archive/Superstock, Inc.; 86: Paula Solloway/Alamy Images; 89: RichardBakerHeathrow/Alamy Images; 90: Stephen Finn/Alamy Images; 92: Press Association/AP Images; 93: Simon Price/Alamy Images; 94: John Pavel/Dreamstime; 96: Pantheon/Superstock, Inc.; 97: The Granger Collection, New York; 98: Hulton Archive/Getty Images; 99: Press Association/AP Images; 100: Marco Secchi/Alamy Images; 101: Fortean/TopFoto/The Image Works; 102: Martin Thomas Photography/Alamy Images; 104: The Art Archive at Art Resource; 106: David Fisher/Rex USA; 107: Susannah Pollen Ltd./Bridgeman Art Library; 108 left: Robert Harding Picture Library/Superstock, Inc.; 108 right: age fotostock/Superstock, Inc.; 109: Dave Tonge/Getty Images; 110: VisitBritain/Andy Sewell/Getty Images; 111: Robbie Jack/Corbis Images; 112: Rob Ball/Getty Images; 113: Express Newspapers/AP Images; 114: Chris Brunskill/BPI/Icon SMI 176/Newscom; 116: Yadid Levy/Alamy Images; 118: neeiillllaangaan/Fotolia; 119: Simon Reddy/Alamy Images; 120: Hlphoto/Dreamstime; 121: Robin Stewart/Shutterstock, Inc.; 122: Monkey Business Images/Dreamstime; 123: Roberto Ricciuti/Getty Images; 125: Pako Mera/Alamy Images; 126: Yadid Levy/Alamy Images; 130: Ivan Vdovin/age fotostock/Superstock, Inc.; 131 top: wavebreakmedia/Shutterstock, Inc.; 131 bottom: Kathleen Norris Cook/Alamy Images; 132 top: Heartland Arts/Shutterstock, Inc.; 132 bottom: Stockcube/Dreamstime; 133 top: Simon Price/Alamy Images; 133 bottom: David Fisher/Rex/Rex USA.

Maps by XNR Productions, Inc.